POL POT

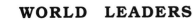

POL POT

Rebecca Stefoff

CHELSEA HOUSE PUBLISHERS
NEW YORK
PHILADELPHIA

Chelsea House Publishers
EDITOR-IN-CHIEF: Remmel Nunn
MANAGING EDITOR: Karyn Gullen Browne
COPY CHIEF: Juliann Barbato
PICTURE EDITOR: Adrian G. Allen
ART DIRECTOR: Maria Epes
DEPUTY COPY CHIEF: Mark Rifkin
ASSISTANT ART DIRECTOR: Loraine Machlin
MANUFACTURING MANAGER: Gerald Levine
SYSTEMS MANAGER: Rachel Vigier
PRODUCTION MANAGER: Joseph Romano
PRODUCTION COORDINATOR: Marie Claire Cebrián

World Leaders—Past & Present
SENIOR EDITOR: John Selfridge

Staff for POL POT
ASSOCIATE EDITOR: Jeff Klein
COPY EDITOR: Philip Koslow
EDITORIAL ASSISTANT: Martin Mooney
PICTURE RESEARCHER: Ken Braun
DESIGNER: James Baker
COVER ILLUSTRATION: Toni Limtaco

First Printing

1 3 5 7 9 8 6 4 2

Library of Congress Cataloging-in-Publication Data

Stefoff, Rebecca.
    Pol Pot/Rebecca Stefoff.
    p.   cm.—(World leaders past & present)
    Includes bibliographical references.
    Summary: A biography of the prime minister of Cambodia.
    ISBN 1-55546-848-9
        0-7910-0683-2 (pbk.)
    1. Pol Pot—Juvenile literature. 2. Prime ministers—Cambodia—
Biography—Juvenile literature. [1. Pol Pot. 2. Prime ministers. 3.
Cambodia—History—1925–]   I. Title. II. Series.
DS554.83.P65S73   1990
959.604'092—dc20   90–1798
[B]   CIP
[92]   AC

Contents

JOHN ADAMS
JOHN QUINCY ADAMS
KONRAD ADENAUER
ALEXANDER THE GREAT
SALVADOR ALLENDE
MARC ANTONY
CORAZON AQUINO
YASIR ARAFAT
KING ARTHUR
HAFEZ al-ASSAD
KEMAL ATATÜRK
ATTILA
CLEMENT ATTLEE
AUGUSTUS CAESAR
MENACHEM BEGIN
DAVID BEN-GURION
OTTO VON BISMARCK
LÉON BLUM
SIMON BOLÍVAR
CESARE BORGIA
WILLY BRANDT
LEONID BREZHNEV
JULIUS CAESAR
JOHN CALVIN
JIMMY CARTER
FIDEL CASTRO
CATHERINE THE GREAT
CHARLEMAGNE
CHIANG KAI-SHEK
WINSTON CHURCHILL
GEORGES CLEMENCEAU
CLEOPATRA
CONSTANTINE THE GREAT
HERNÁN CORTÉS
OLIVER CROMWELL
GEORGES-JACQUES
  DANTON
JEFFERSON DAVIS
MOSHE DAYAN
CHARLES DE GAULLE
EAMON DE VALERA
EUGENE DEBS
DENG XIAOPING
BENJAMIN DISRAELI
ALEXANDER DUBČEK
FRANÇOIS & JEAN-CLAUDE
  DUVALIER
DWIGHT EISENHOWER
ELEANOR OF AQUITAINE
ELIZABETH I
FAISAL
FERDINAND & ISABELLA
FRANCISCO FRANCO
BENJAMIN FRANKLIN

FREDERICK THE GREAT
INDIRA GANDHI
MOHANDAS GANDHI
GIUSEPPE GARIBALDI
AMIN & BASHIR GEMAYEL
GENGHIS KHAN
WILLIAM GLADSTONE
MIKHAIL GORBACHEV
ULYSSES S. GRANT
ERNESTO "CHE" GUEVARA
TENZIN GYATSO
ALEXANDER HAMILTON
DAG HAMMARSKJÖLD
HENRY VIII
HENRY OF NAVARRE
PAUL VON HINDENBURG
HIROHITO
ADOLF HITLER
HO CHI MINH
KING HUSSEIN
IVAN THE TERRIBLE
ANDREW JACKSON
JAMES I
WOJCIECH JARUZELSKI
THOMAS JEFFERSON
JOAN OF ARC
POPE JOHN XXIII
POPE JOHN PAUL II
LYNDON JOHNSON
BENITO JUÁREZ
JOHN KENNEDY
ROBERT KENNEDY
JOMO KENYATTA
AYATOLLAH KHOMEINI
NIKITA KHRUSHCHEV
KIM IL SUNG
MARTIN LUTHER KING, JR.
HENRY KISSINGER
KUBLAI KHAN
LAFAYETTE
ROBERT E. LEE
VLADIMIR LENIN
ABRAHAM LINCOLN
DAVID LLOYD GEORGE
LOUIS XIV
MARTIN LUTHER
JUDAS MACCABEUS
JAMES MADISON
NELSON & WINNIE
  MANDELA
MAO ZEDONG
FERDINAND MARCOS
GEORGE MARSHALL

MARY, QUEEN OF SCOTS
TOMÁŠ MASARYK
GOLDA MEIR
KLEMENS VON METTERNICH
JAMES MONROE
HOSNI MUBARAK
ROBERT MUGABE
BENITO MUSSOLINI
NAPOLÉON BONAPARTE
GAMAL ABDEL NASSER
JAWAHARLAL NEHRU
NERO
NICHOLAS II
RICHARD NIXON
KWAME NKRUMAH
DANIEL ORTEGA
MOHAMMED REZA PAHLAVI
THOMAS PAINE
CHARLES STEWART
  PARNELL
PERICLES
JUAN PERÓN
PETER THE GREAT
POL POT
MUAMMAR EL-QADDAFI
RONALD REAGAN
CARDINAL RICHELIEU
MAXIMILIEN ROBESPIERRE
ELEANOR ROOSEVELT
FRANKLIN ROOSEVELT
THEODORE ROOSEVELT
ANWAR SADAT
HAILE SELASSIE
PRINCE SIHANOUK
JAN SMUTS
JOSEPH STALIN
SUKARNO
SUN YAT-SEN
TAMERLANE
MOTHER TERESA
MARGARET THATCHER
JOSIP BROZ TITO
TOUSSAINT L'OUVERTURE
LEON TROTSKY
PIERRE TRUDEAU
HARRY TRUMAN
QUEEN VICTORIA
LECH WALESA
GEORGE WASHINGTON
CHAIM WEIZMANN
WOODROW WILSON
XERXES
EMILIANO ZAPATA
ZHOU ENLAI

CHELSEA HOUSE PUBLISHERS

ON LEADERSHIP

Arthur M. Schlesinger, jr.

LEADERSHIP, it may be said, is really what makes the world go round. Love no doubt smooths the passage; but love is a private transaction between consenting adults. Leadership is a public transaction with history. The idea of leadership affirms the capacity of individuals to move, inspire, and mobilize masses of people so that they act together in pursuit of an end. Sometimes leadership serves good purposes, sometimes bad; but whether the end is benign or evil, great leaders are those men and women who leave their personal stamp on history.

Now, the very concept of leadership implies the proposition that individuals can make a difference. This proposition has never been universally accepted. From classical times to the present day, eminent thinkers have regarded individuals as no more than the agents and pawns of larger forces, whether the gods and goddesses of the ancient world or, in the modern era, race, class, nation, the dialectic, the will of the people, the spirit of the times, history itself. Against such forces, the individual dwindles into insignificance.

So contends the thesis of historical determinism. Tolstoy's great novel *War and Peace* offers a famous statement of the case. Why, Tolstoy asked, did millions of men in the Napoleonic Wars, denying their human feelings and their common sense, move back and forth across Europe slaughtering their fellows? "The war," Tolstoy answered, "was bound to happen simply because it was bound to happen." All prior history predetermined it. As for leaders, they, Tolstoy said, "are but the labels that serve to give a name to an end and, like labels, they have the least possible connection with the event." The greater the leader, "the more conspicuous the inevitability and the predestination of every act he commits." The leader, said Tolstoy, is "the slave of history."

Determinism takes many forms. Marxism is the determinism of class. Nazism the determinism of race. But the idea of men and women as the slaves of history runs athwart the deepest human instincts. Rigid determinism abolishes the idea of human freedom—

the assumption of free choice that underlies every move we make, every word we speak, every thought we think. It abolishes the idea of human responsibility, since it is manifestly unfair to reward or punish people for actions that are by definition beyond their control. No one can live consistently by any deterministic creed. The Marxist states prove this themselves by their extreme susceptibility to the cult of leadership.

More than that, history refutes the idea that individuals make no difference. In December 1931 a British politician crossing Park Avenue in New York City between 76th and 77th Streets around 10:30 P.M. looked in the wrong direction and was knocked down by an automobile—a moment, he later recalled, of a man aghast, a world aglare: "I do not understand why I was not broken like an eggshell or squashed like a gooseberry." Fourteen months later an American politician, sitting in an open car in Miami, Florida, was fired on by an assassin; the man beside him was hit. Those who believe that individuals make no difference to history might well ponder whether the next two decades would have been the same had Mario Constasino's car killed Winston Churchill in 1931 and Giuseppe Zangara's bullet killed Franklin Roosevelt in 1933. Suppose, in addition, that Adolf Hitler had been killed in the street fighting during the Munich *Putsch* of 1923 and that Lenin had died of typhus during World War I. What would the 20th century be like now?

For better or for worse, individuals do make a difference. "The notion that a people can run itself and its affairs anonymously," wrote the philosopher William James, "is now well known to be the silliest of absurdities. Mankind does nothing save through initiatives on the part of inventors, great or small, and imitation by the rest of us—these are the sole factors in human progress. Individuals of genius show the way, and set the patterns, which common people then adopt and follow."

Leadership, James suggests, means leadership in thought as well as in action. In the long run, leaders in thought may well make the greater difference to the world. But, as Woodrow Wilson once said, "Those only are leaders of men, in the general eye, who lead in action. . . . It is at their hands that new thought gets its translation into the crude language of deeds." Leaders in thought often invent in solitude and obscurity, leaving to later generations the tasks of imitation. Leaders in action—the leaders portrayed in this series—have to be effective in their own time.

And they cannot be effective by themselves. They must act in response to the rhythms of their age. Their genius must be adapted, in a phrase of William James's, "to the receptivities of the moment." Leaders are useless without followers. "There goes the mob," said the French politician hearing a clamor in the streets. "I am their leader. I must follow them." Great leaders turn the inchoate emotions of the mob to purposes of their own. They seize on the opportunities of their time, the hopes, fears, frustrations, crises, potentialities. They succeed when events have prepared the way for them, when the community is awaiting to be aroused, when they can provide the clarifying and organizing ideas. Leadership ignites the circuit between the individual and the mass and thereby alters history.

It may alter history for better or for worse. Leaders have been responsible for the most extravagant follies and most monstrous crimes that have beset suffering humanity. They have also been vital in such gains as humanity has made in individual freedom, religious and racial tolerance, social justice, and respect for human rights.

There is no sure way to tell in advance who is going to lead for good and who for evil. But a glance at the gallery of men and women in *World Leaders—Past and Present* suggests some useful tests.

One test is this: Do leaders lead by force or by persuasion? By command or by consent? Through most of history leadership was exercised by the divine right of authority. The duty of followers was to defer and to obey. "Theirs not to reason why / Theirs but to do and die." On occasion, as with the so-called enlightened despots of the 18th century in Europe, absolutist leadership was animated by humane purposes. More often, absolutism nourished the passion for domination, land, gold, and conquest and resulted in tyranny.

The great revolution of modern times has been the revolution of equality. The idea that all people should be equal in their legal condition has undermined the old structure of authority, hierarchy, and deference. The revolution of equality has had two contrary effects on the nature of leadership. For equality, as Alexis de Tocqueville pointed out in his great study *Democracy in America*, might mean equality in servitude as well as equality in freedom.

"I know of only two methods of establishing equality in the political world," Tocqueville wrote. "Rights must be given to every citizen, or none at all to anyone . . . save one, who is the master of all." There was no middle ground "between the sovereignty of all and the absolute power of one man." In his astonishing prediction of 20th-century totalitarian dictatorship, Tocqueville explained how the revolution of equality could lead to the *"Führerprinzip"* and more terrible absolutism than the world had ever known.

But when rights are given to every citizen and the sovereignty of all is established, the problem of leadership takes a new form, becomes more exacting than ever before. It is easy to issue commands and enforce them by the rope and the stake, the concentration camp and the *gulag.* It is much harder to use argument and achievement to overcome opposition and win consent. The Founding Fathers of the United States understood the difficulty. They believed that history had given them the opportunity to decide, as Alexander Hamilton wrote in the first Federalist Paper, whether men are indeed capable of basing government on "reflection and choice, or whether they are forever destined to depend . . . on accident and force."

Government by reflection and choice called for a new style of leadership and a new quality of followership. It required leaders to be responsive to popular concerns, and it required followers to be active and informed participants in the process. Democracy does not eliminate emotion from politics; sometimes it fosters demagoguery; but it is confident that, as the greatest of democratic leaders put it, you cannot fool all of the people all of the time. It measures leadership by results and retires those who overreach or falter or fail.

It is true that in the long run despots are measured by results too. But they can postpone the day of judgment, sometimes indefinitely, and in the meantime they can do infinite harm. It is also true that democracy is no guarantee of virtue and intelligence in government, for the voice of the people is not necessarily the voice of God. But democracy, by assuring the right of opposition, offers built-in resistance to the evils inherent in absolutism. As the theologian Reinhold Niebuhr summed it up, "Man's capacity for justice makes democracy possible, but man's inclination to injustice makes democracy necessary."

A second test for leadership is the end for which power is sought. When leaders have as their goal the supremacy of a master race or the promotion of totalitarian revolution or the acquisition and exploitation of colonies or the protection of greed and privilege or the preservation of personal power, it is likely that their leadership will do little to advance the cause of humanity. When their goal is the abolition of slavery, the liberation of women, the enlargement of opportunity for the poor and powerless, the extension of equal rights to racial minorities, the defense of the freedoms of expression and opposition, it is likely that their leadership will increase the sum of human liberty and welfare.

Leaders have done great harm to the world. They have also conferred great benefits. You will find both sorts in this series. Even "good" leaders must be regarded with a certain wariness. Leaders are not demigods; they put on their trousers one leg after another just like ordinary mortals. No leader is infallible, and every leader needs to be reminded of this at regular intervals. Irreverence irritates leaders but is their salvation. Unquestioning submission corrupts leaders and demeans followers. Making a cult of a leader is always a mistake. Fortunately hero worship generates its own antidote. "Every hero," said Emerson, "becomes a bore at last."

The signal benefit the great leaders confer is to embolden the rest of us to live according to our own best selves, to be active, insistent, and resolute in affirming our own sense of things. For great leaders attest to the reality of human freedom against the supposed inevitabilities of history. And they attest to the wisdom and power that may lie within the most unlikely of us, which is why Abraham Lincoln remains the supreme example of great leadership. A great leader, said Emerson, exhibits new possibilities to all humanity. "We feed on genius. . . . Great men exist that there may be greater men."

Great leaders, in short, justify themselves by emancipating and empowering their followers. So humanity struggles to master its destiny, remembering with Alexis de Tocqueville: "It is true that around every man a fatal circle is traced beyond which he cannot pass; but within the wide verge of that circle he is powerful and free; as it is with man, so with communities."

1
The Fall of Phnom Penh

In 1974, Phnom Penh was a city under siege. It was the power base of the government of Cambodia, a small country in the heart of Southeast Asia. That government, headed by General Lon Nol and supported by military and financial aid from the United States, was struggling to survive against the assault of the Communist Khmer Rouge army that controlled an ever-increasing share of the countryside. As the year wore on, the Khmer Rouge moved closer to Phnom Penh every day, and the city seethed with rumors, uncertainty, excitement, and fear. Phnom Penh was both the capital and the only large city in Cambodia; everyone knew that its fate would determine that of the nation.

Phnom Penh had occupied a central role in Cambodian life and politics for five centuries. According to legend, the site that is now occupied by Phnom Penh, at the junction of the Mekong and Bassac rivers in the south-central part of the country, was once a small village. There, centuries ago, a mighty flood washed a tree into the house of a woman named Penh, who lived on a hill in the village. In the hollow trunk of the tree, Penh found four bronze statues of Buddha, the founder of Buddhism, which

> *It surprises me now, but most of us pretended that life was almost normal. We made ourselves believe that Phnom Penh was a little island of peace and that it was going to stay that way.*
> —HAING NGOR
> former resident of Phnom Penh and Cambodian refugeee

Civilians in the Cambodian capital of Phnom Penh flee rebel mortar fire as a government soldier ducks for cover in February 1975. Two months later the Communist rebels, or Khmer Rouge, marched into the city, ending a long, bloody civil war — and initiating the still bloodier regime of Pol Pot.

has been the principal religion of Cambodia since the 13th century. Penh built a *wat*, or temple, to house the statues. Throngs of pilgrims came there to worship, and the village grew in importance and was given its present name, which means "the hill of lady Penh." In 1431, when enemies from Siam (present-day Thailand) invaded Cambodia and seized the former capital city of Angkor Thom, the king made Phnom Penh his new capital. Phnom Penh eventually fell to the Siamese in 1594, but the city's worst agonies are much more recent.

In the 1960s, Phnom Penh was something of a Southeast Asian showplace. The French, who had administered Cambodia as a protectorate from 1862 to 1953, had built wide, European-style paved boulevards that were shaded with rows of sugar palms. They had also constructed some impressive buildings in the French manner, with stone facades and arched windows; these included hotels, government offices, theaters, and an opera house. Nightclubs and casinos catered to tourists and foreign diplomats alike.

Yet the city remained predominantly Asian. Its skyline was defined by pagoda roofs, with their upcurling eaves and ornamented tiles, and by the distinctive layered, cone-shaped towers of traditional Cambodian architecture. Rickshas and *kong dup* (bicycle taxis) crowded the streets; the riverfront was full of the Chinese-style cargo vessels called junks and the smaller, flat-bottomed boats called sampans that carried goods along the Mekong River from Luang Prabang in Laos to the delta in South Vietnam; and the city's huge and ancient open-air market, the Tuol Tumpuong, was one of the liveliest in all of Asia. Under the government of Prince Norodom Sihanouk, who had once ruled as king but had stepped down from his throne to assume the post of prime minister, Cambodia presented to the world a picture of peaceful prosperity, with Phnom Penh as the symbol of commerce and culture.

That picture began to change in the late 1960s, when opposition to Sihanouk's despotic rule gained strength throughout the country. Cambodia was torn by internal strife, government repression,

guerrilla movements, and finally open civil war. During the same period, the war raging in Vietnam, Cambodia's neighbor to the east, spilled over the borders into Cambodia, which was drawn into the widening conflict in Southeast Asia. The picture was altered dramatically in 1970, when a coup d'état led by Lon Nol deposed Sihanouk, drove him into exile, and set up a new regime called the Khmer Republic. And in 1974, as the Khmer Rouge sought to wrest control of the capital from the Khmer Republic, Phnom Penh and all of Cambodia stood on the threshold of still more changes — upheavals that would transform the capital into a ghost city strewn with corpses and the country into a horrific labor camp.

The people of Phnom Penh knew nothing of this in 1974. For the most part, they tried to go about their business as usual. But as the year wore on,

A Phnom Penh street in the late 1950s, with portions of the royal palace complex in the background. Until the bloodshed and warfare of the 1970s the city was famous for its beauty and gentility.

life in the city gradually assumed a nightmarish air of unreality. Armed Khmer Republic soldiers were everywhere. Sensing troubled times ahead, those citizens who could afford it stockpiled weapons of their own: pistols, old shotguns once used by foreign sportsmen for duck hunting in the marshes, Chinese-made AK-47 automatic rifles smuggled in from the Vietnamese Communists, or U.S.-made M16s purchased on the black market from Lon Nol's soldiers. Many members of the city's affluent, educated elite fled the country or sent their children and their gold beyond the borders for safety. Some of those who remained began to hoard gold and jewelry to use in barter if the money economy broke down; many accumulated stores of medicine and rice in the expectation of shortages.

Perhaps the single biggest change in Phnom Penh was in the number of its inhabitants. At the time of the Lon Nol coup in 1970, the capital's population was well under 1 million — most estimates put it between 600,000 and 750,000. Soon after the coup, however, peasant farmers and villagers from the outlying rural provinces began trickling into the city to escape the fighting between the Khmer Republic and Khmer Rouge forces — and also to escape the

A Cambodian villager weeps near the ruins of his home in the aftermath of 1974 fighting south of Phnom Penh. Hundreds of thousands were killed in the five years of full-scale civil war between the government and Pol Pot's Khmer Rouge.

widespread and destructive bombing of the Cambodian countryside by the United States in support of its ally, Lon Nol. The trickle of refugees became a stream and then a flood. By 1974, Phnom Penh's population had quadrupled to 2.5 million or more, out of the country's total population of 7.3 million. Many of the refugees were taken in by family members or friends in Phnom Penh, but hundreds of thousands established themselves in sprawling shantytowns along the river and at the edges of the city. Streets, markets, and shops were crammed to capacity; water and electrical service began to fail; and stories told by the refugees fueled the growing mood of apprehension.

Few residents of Phnom Penh had any clear idea of what the fighting was about. Most of them had at least one friend or relative in the Khmer Rouge army, and many despised the openly corrupt and violent Lon Nol regime and hoped for better government under the Khmer Rouge. Furthermore, Prince Sihanouk, who was still revered and regarded as their leader by many Cambodians, had allied himself with the Khmer Rouge — even though he and they had been enemies in the late 1960s. To many Cambodians, however, this alliance seemed to mean that once the Khmer Rouge had overthrown Lon Nol's Khmer Republic, the country would return to its prewar state, with a government headed by Sihanouk. A good many of these Cambodians were unaware that the Khmer Rouge army was controlled and officered by high-ranking members of the Communist Party of Kampuchea (CPK); they viewed the Khmer Rouge soldiers as nationalists and freedom fighters.

Sometimes, people can appear as very gentle, very innocent. Pol Pot is very charming, very innocent. His face, his behavior even, is very polite, but he is very, very cruel.
—PRINCE NORODOM SIHANOUK
Cambodian ruler

Others were not so optimistic. Many of the more affluent urban Cambodians were linked with Lon Nol or supported his regime. These people — mostly army officers, bureaucrats, and merchants who supplied goods to the army — had profited greatly through bribery and graft during the Khmer Republic years and dreaded a reversal of their fortunes. But most accounts suggest that the largest portion of the city's population was politically neutral, favoring neither the Khmer Republic nor the Khmer

Rouge, simply hoping for an end to the war so that they could get on with their lives. These neutrals were deeply disturbed by the rumors that spread through Phnom Penh: that Lon Nol practiced evil witchcraft, that his soldiers were murdering peasants in the south, and that the Khmer Rouge guerrillas destroyed temples and tortured prisoners to death. The city buzzed with speculation. Would the Lon Nol regime hold? Would the Khmer Rouge take over? What then?

Meanwhile, the Khmer Rouge tightened the noose around Phnom Penh. At the beginning of 1974, the major roads into and out of the city were held by Khmer Rouge forces. In January, artillery shells began falling on the city; in the first round of shelling, 10,000 homes were destroyed, and hundreds of people were killed. In February, the Khmer Republic troops managed to push their attackers back from the perimeter of the city. They had learned, however, that the Khmer Rouge fought with extraordinary tenacity and were willing to accept enormous losses in battle. In one engagement west of the city, for example, the Khmer Rouge lost 380 men to 35 on the Lon Nol side.

Their willingness to advance at all costs gained ground for the Khmer Rouge. By late spring, they held enough positions along the Mekong River to disrupt boat traffic into and out of Phnom Penh, thus limiting both military and civilian supplies to the capital. In November, the Khmer Rouge engaged the Khmer Republic in a major battle northeast of the city. At a cost of 588 dead to the republic's 16, the Khmer Rouge had taken territory that nearly closed the circle around Phnom Penh.

On January 1, 1975, the Khmer Rouge army launched a final, all-out attack on the city. The rebels placed scores of floating mines in the Mekong River, halting all river traffic, and repeatedly shelled Pochentong, the city's chief airport. The city was ringed with smoke by day and flame by night. Its citizens became accustomed to the thud of Khmer Rouge artillery fire and the drone of Khmer Republic jets. Foreigners and wealthy Cambodians flocked to the airport to vie for seats on departing planes.

The pace of events accelerated. On April 1, Lon Nol's own military officers and U.S. advisers convinced him to leave Cambodia, hoping that his departure would lead to peace negotiations between the Khmer Rouge and the Khmer Republic. Lon Nol retreated to a hospital in Hawaii, but no peace negotiations resulted, for the Khmer Rouge sensed victory. That same day, Khmer Rouge forces captured Neak Luong, a port on the Mekong south of Phnom Penh that was one of the remaining strongholds of Lon Nol's forces.

On April 12, the U.S. embassy was shut down, its personnel and their families flown by helicopter to Thailand. Some American journalists stayed on for a few days or weeks to cover the coming events. (One of them was Sydney Schanberg, then writing for the *New York Times*; his Cambodian assistant, Dith Pran, would undergo a long, terrifying ordeal at the hands of the Khmer Rouge that was later chronicled in the award-winning film *The Killing Fields*.) Other embassies remained open, but few foreigners

One of the first Khmer Rouge guerrillas to march into Phnom Penh on April 17, 1975, brandishes a flag and an assault rifle as his comrades begin to round up the city's residents for removal to labor camps in the countryside.

19

A rare photo of Pol Pot, the shadowy leader of the Khmer Rouge and prime minister of Democratic Kampuchea — as he renamed Cambodia — from 1975 to 1979. His regime killed 1 million to 2 million Cambodians, out of a total population of 7 million, by execution, overwork, starvation, and torture.

and almost no Americans were seen on the streets of Phnom Penh at this time.

On April 15, the Khmer Rouge captured Takhmau, an outlying village and the last bastion of the Khmer Republic army. The next day, the remaining Khmer Republic officials sent a telegram to Prince Sihanouk in Beijing, China, offering to surrender to him in exchange for a cease-fire. Early in the morning of April 17, Sihanouk sent back a refusal. He may have wanted to accept the offer, but he had long since lost all control over the Khmer Rouge, who now refused to negotiate with the Khmer Republic.

At 8:30 that morning, after receiving Sihanouk's telegram, the Khmer Republic leaders gathered at a sports stadium, where a helicopter fleet awaited them. They planned to evacuate the city and flee to northern Cambodia, where they could set up a government-in-exile and continue the war against the Khmer Rouge. Most of the helicopters had engine trouble, though, and could not take off. Only a few officials escaped; the rest were stranded in the city.

Later in the morning, the troops of the Khmer Rouge marched into Phnom Penh. They met little opposition. Most of the Khmer Republic soldiers were too dispirited or too fearful to put up a fight. The streets were empty, because the civilian population was waiting indoors to see what would happen.

One of the first to discover what his future would be under the Khmer Rouge was Long Boret, the prime minister of the Khmer Republic; he had failed to escape Phnom Penh in time. Long Boret was captured by the Khmer Rouge, sentenced to death, and executed at once; it is said that he was beheaded on the lawn of an exclusive country club that had been patronized by Lon Nol's followers.

On April 23, after the city had been in Khmer Rouge hands for six days, a jeep entered Phnom Penh. In it rode the new leader of Cambodia. No parade ushered him into the fallen capital, and no fanfare greeted his arrival. Most of his followers did not even know that this soft-spoken, round-faced man was the military commander and mastermind of the Khmer Rouge. He had long made a practice of shrouding his identity and his activities in secrecy, and it would be more than a year after the fall of Phnom Penh before he emerged publicly as the head of the new government of Cambodia, which he called Democratic Kampuchea. Only a handful of his most trusted intimates knew that his name was Saloth Sar.

Since his student days, Saloth Sar had used aliases and pseudonyms to conceal his identity. Now, upon arriving in Phnom Penh, he gave himself the nom de guerre Pol Pot. It was by this name that he would soon become known to the world as revolutionary, prime minister, dictator, and genocidal mass murderer.

Pol Pot's actions from 1975 to 1979, when between 1 million and 2 million Cambodians died under his rule in Democratic Kampuchea, have been the subject of extensive examination. In a few years, he wrought enormous destruction and gave rise to a new word — *autogenocide*, meaning the mass killing of one's own people. He became one of the most feared and reviled world leaders in modern history. Yet he is also perhaps the most secretive head of state the world has ever seen. Little is known about the man himself. His life, like the motives that compelled him to create a regime of intimidation and torture in Cambodia, remains largely a mystery.

The last time I saw the airport, in April 1975, it was under heavy rocket attack from the Khmer Rouge as the Americans pulled out; it was all smoke and noise and fear and confusion.
—DITH PRAN
Cambodian refugee, upon returning to Phnom Penh in 1989

2
The Broken Empire

There is a traditional Cambodian expression: "Between the tiger and the crocodile." Its basic meaning is obvious — to be in a difficult position. But the Cambodian saying has a geographic and historical meaning, too. In this sense, it describes the position that the Cambodian people feel they have occupied for centuries, sandwiched between two larger, more powerful nations, Thailand and Vietnam. A long history of conflict with the tiger on the west and the crocodile on the east has given the Cambodians a profound fear of being overrun, of being abolished as a people.

Cambodia is a land of 69,898 square miles (183,132 square kilometers). It is bordered on the west and northwest by Thailand, on the north by Laos, and on the east and southeast by Vietnam; in the southwest is its only outlet to the sea, a stretch of coastline on the Gulf of Siam. Cambodia's principal waterways are the Mekong River, which runs through the country from north to south, and the Bassac River in the south.

An Ancestral prophecy predicts that one day the unfortunate Khmer people will be forced to choose between being eaten by tigers or swallowed by crocodiles. Today we are seeing that prophecy fulfilled in the most tragic way possible.
—PRINCE NORODOM SIHANOUK
Cambodian ruler, in 1980

Peasants work a rice paddy near the South Vietnamese border in the early 1960s. Cambodia, deeply traditional and rich agriculturally, was for centuries caught in struggles between its more populous and powerful neighbors, Vietnam and Thailand.

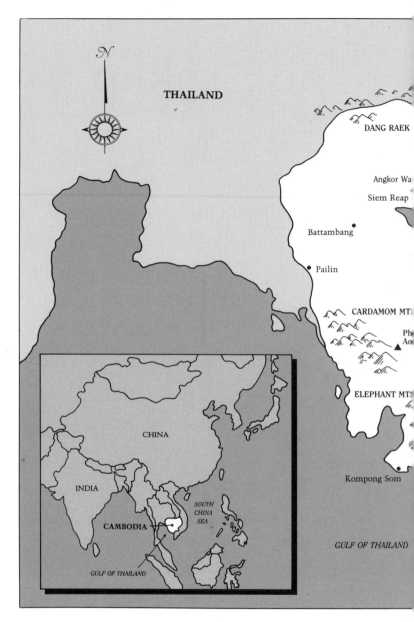

THAILAND

DANG RAEK

Angkor Wa

Siem Reap

Battambang

Pailin

CARDAMOM MT

Ph
Ao

ELEPHANT MT'

Kompong Som

GULF OF THAILAND

CHINA

INDIA

SOUTH
CHINA
SEA

CAMBODIA

GULF OF THAILAND

For centuries Cambodia, a country the size of Missouri, has endured repeated invasions and occupations by its two larger and more powerful neighbors, Thailand and Vietnam. Many Cambodians are of Vietnamese, Thai, or Chinese ancestry.

The center of the country is a flat, fertile region, noted for rice growing and for the presence of a large lake, the Tonle Sap, which is one of the world's richest freshwater fisheries. Traditionally, central Cambodia has been the most densely populated part of the country. Around this plain, the land rises gradually to a hilly region of grasslands and scattered

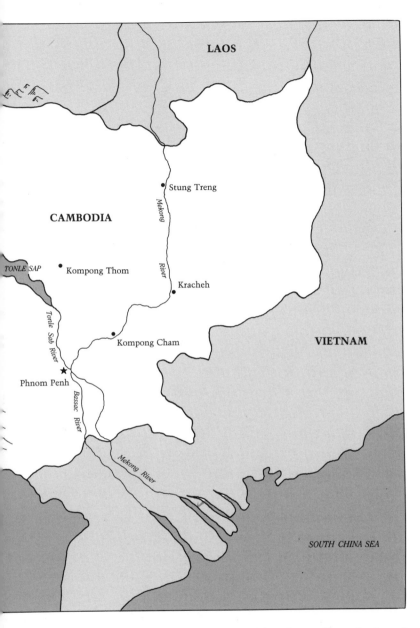

forests. Beyond this region, like the sides of a bowl containing the central lowland, is a ring of jungle-covered mountains that separate central Cambodia from the coastal plain and from the surrounding countries. These mountain districts form the least densely populated part of the country, although some small cities and towns are found there. The

A 12th-century bas-relief depicts a Khmer king leading his army to conquest. From the 9th to the 15th century, the Khmer Empire, the predecessor of modern Cambodia, was the predominant force in Southeast Asia.

mountains have traditionally been the home of hill tribes that lived in isolation and had little contact with the mainstream of Cambodian culture; in recent years, the hard-to-reach jungle villages and camps in the mountains have also served as bases for the Khmer Rouge and other guerrilla and resistance groups.

The climate is tropical. Daytime temperatures average 95 degrees Fahrenheit in the summer and 82 in the winter. The key factor in Cambodia's weather is the monsoon, a seasonal wind that blows from the southwest and brings torrential rains nearly every day from May to October. As a result, the country has two seasons, wet and dry. The rhythm of life — of planting and harvesting, of religious ritual — has always been shaped by the monsoon. During the almost constant war that has convulsed Cambodia since 1970, the seasons have had a military meaning as well: From November to April, during the dry season, the roads are passable, and army troops that have trucks and heavy guns take to the field. But during the wet season, when roads are flooded and the countryside turns to mud, guerrilla forces that travel on foot and use hand-held weapons have the advantage. Warfare thus takes on a seasonal, turnabout quality in Cambodia.

The majority of Cambodia's people belong to the ethnic group called Khmer and speak the Khmer language. Several thousand years ago, peoples from the island groups that are now called Malaysia and

Indonesia migrated northward into the Southeast Asian peninsula. There they encountered nomadic groups that had moved south from Tibet and China. Over time, the blending of these peoples in present-day Cambodia gave rise to the Khmer. Before 1970, the country also had a sizable population of ethnic Vietnamese, Chinese, Burmese, and Chams (a Muslim people of Vietnamese-Malaysian descent who were concentrated in the southern part of the country). Persecution and purges by successive regimes have greatly reduced these ethnic minorities.

The history of the Khmer is fairly well documented from about the 1st century A.D., when a Khmer empire called Funan arose in Cambodia. Many elements of Funanese culture — such as temple architecture, dances, and cooking styles — were borrowed or adapted from India, and even today the Indian heritage is noticeable in Cambodian art and architecture. India also shared with the Khmer its two great religions, Hinduism and Buddhism.

By the early 6th century, Funan had grown strong enough to dominate two neighboring states, Chenla in present-day Thailand and Champa in present-day southern Vietnam. In 598, a Khmer king united Funan and Chenla in a single empire, which was called Chenla, but bickering among members of the royal family caused Chenla to disintegrate in the 7th century. At the same time, the rulers of Java, an island kingdom in what is now Indonesia, intermarried with Khmer royalty.

In the 8th century, Khmer princes arrived in Cambodia from Java and established a state that was to be the greatest power in the region for centuries. This state was called Kambuja, from which the modern names Cambodia and Kampuchea come; it is also called the Khmer Empire.

The first great Khmer ruler was Jayavarman II, who became king in 802. One of his acts was to have a lasting effect on Cambodian culture, reaching all the way to the politics of the 20th century. Jayavarman declared himself *deva-raja*, or god-king — that is, a ruler who was a god (*deva*) as well as a king (*raja*). From that time on, the Khmer rulers were considered by their subjects to be deities as well as earthly leaders and were worshiped as

A portion of the Angkor Wat temple complex, considered one of the architectural wonders of the world. Built during the height of the Khmer Empire, the complex reflects the combination of Buddhist, Hindu, and local beliefs that marked Khmer religion.

French colonial officers lead Indochinese troops in 1905 in the hilly grasslands of northern Vietnam. In the second half of the 19th century, France annexed Vietnam, Cambodia, and Laos, uniting them under a single administration as French Indochina.

such. During much of his political career, Prince Sihanouk enjoyed playing the part of the god-king and benefited from the reverence accorded him by the Cambodian people.

Beginning around 1130, the Khmer rulers constructed a series of monumental temples at a site called Angkor in the north-central part of Cambodia, not far from the Tonle Sap. Dedicated at first to Hindu deities and later to Buddha, these temples form a massive, sprawling complex that is called Angkor Wat. An immense capital city called Angkor Thom was built nearby by King Jayavarman VII, who held the throne from 1181 to about 1215. Under his rule, the Khmer Empire reached its greatest extent. It included all of modern Cambodia as well as much of Thailand and parts of Laos, Vietnam, and Malaysia.

In the 13th and 14th centuries, however, the power of the Khmer Empire began to erode. Khmer territory in what is now Laos was taken from the empire by a Laotian kingdom called Lan Xang. After years of fighting, the people of Annam, or northern Vietnam, pushed south and seized Champa, which remained in Vietnamese hands thereafter. This struggle was to have a long-lasting effect on the Khmer people, who have regarded the Mekong Delta as theirs by right ever since and have never ceased to resent the Vietnamese encroachment. Even today, centuries after the Vietnamese conquest of Champa, many Cambodians automatically refer to southern Vietnam as Kampuchea Krom, or "lower Cambodia."

The worst blow to the tottering Khmer Empire came in 1431, when the Siamese invaded Kambuja and sacked Angkor. Cambodian history over the next three centuries resembles a complicated balancing act by which the Khmer kings constantly struggled to keep their nation from being overwhelmed by their more powerful neighbors. The Khmers sought the help of the Siamese against the Vietnamese; then, when the Siamese had grown too demanding, they asked for the help of the Vietnamese against the Siamese.

This system was effective but very costly. The Khmers had to pay for support with land, workers, or goods — and both Siam and Vietnam preferred land. So each time the king of Cambodia sought an alliance, his country grew smaller. In the 17th century, one king was forced to pay tribute to Vietnam and to allow Vietnamese to settle at will in the southern part of Cambodia. In turn, his successor, hoping to drive out the Vietnamese with Siamese help, was forced to give Siam the two important provinces of Battambang (site of several ruby mines) and Siem Reap (which includes Angkor); these provinces were not returned to Cambodia until 1907.

This seesaw pattern continued for several centuries. By the middle of the 19th century, Cambodia was a puppet kingdom whose rulers owed allegiance to both Siam and Vietnam. At this point the politics of the region shifted in favor of the French, who were busily establishing territorial claims throughout Southeast Asia in the hope of matching the wealth and influence that the British had gained through their control of India and Burma.

In 1862, the French presence had become sufficiently strong in Vietnam that France was able to pressure the Vietnamese king into signing a treaty that allowed French troops on Southeast Asian soil. France soon learned that the Vietnamese court claimed the allegiance of the Cambodian court; to

The contrast is striking between a glorious past, an insouciant and gay present, and a future—in all probability—disastrous.
—VIRGINIA THOMAS
American historian, describing the Khmer people, in 1937

King Norodom Sihanouk, shortly after being crowned monarch of Cambodia in 1941. Just 18 years old, Sihanouk was selected for the throne by the French because they believed he would prove pliable to French demands. Instead, Sihanouk led his nation on a peaceful but vehement struggle for independence.

the French, then, Cambodia seemed almost like part of Vietnam. And from the French territorial capital at Saigon, in southern Vietnam, Cambodia was only a short journey up the Mekong River. Eager to annex new territory, the French sent diplomats and government representatives to Phnom Penh. Within months, King Norodom of Cambodia — hoping that the French would protect what remained of his country from Siam and Vietnam — had signed a treaty that made Cambodia a protectorate of France. This meant essentially that Norodom ruled the country only as long as the French permitted him to do so and that France controlled Cambodia's international relations. Cambodia became a full colony of France, subject to French law and completely under French administration, in 1884. Like the concept of the deva-raja and the long feud over Kampuchea Krom, French colonialism helped shape modern Cambodian political attitudes. The French claimed to be helping Cambodia develop into a modern nation by building schools, hospitals, and roads and by improving agriculture and industry. Yet critics of the colonial enterprise pointed out that the profits from French sugar plantations and other enterprises in Cambodia went to French landowners and tax collectors, not to the Cambodian people. During the 20th century, as nationalism gained strength around the world and the grip of colonialism loosened little by little, Cambodians increasingly resented French domination of their homeland. Led by a small but vocal group of educated urban Cambodians and by Buddhist monks who feared that the French Catholic influence was eroding the country's traditional religion, a Cambodian independence movement began to take shape.

One of the breeding grounds of the movement was an institution called the Buddhist Institute in Phnom Penh. Ironically, it was established by the French to promote the study of Buddhism and Cambodian culture. French scholars and archaeologists also probed into Cambodian history. They explored and excavated the ruins at Angkor, which had been buried by the jungle and almost forgotten, and they compiled accounts of the Angkorian kings and the glories of the Khmer Empire. These studies led to a rebirth of national pride among the Cambodian people and thus contributed to the growing sentiment that Cambodia ought to be free to stand on its own.

In the decade before the Buddhist Institute was founded in 1930, two men were born who would be deeply affected by the independence movement that it fostered. Sometimes enemies, sometimes allies, between them these two have written much of Cambodia's modern history. One of them, born in 1922 in the royal palace in Phnom Penh, was Prince Norodom Sihanouk, who became king in 1941 and has navigated the troubled waters of Cambodian politics for half a century since then.

The other was Saloth Sar, who became Pol Pot.

The country even had its own annual miracle. The Tonle Sap River changes its course every August, flowing upstream half the year, downstream the other half.
—ELIZABETH BECKER
American journalist

3

Saloth Sar

Neither the date nor the place of Saloth Sar's birth is known with absolute certainty. The vagueness that surrounds his early life is due to two factors: first, the casual attitude toward record keeping that prevailed in rural Cambodia in the first part of the century; and second, Saloth Sar's own habitual secretiveness, which has clouded his past with reticence, evasions, and misinformation.

It seems fairly certain, however, that Saloth Sar was born on May 19 in either 1925 or 1928; most sources agree on 1928. Although some French historians give his place of birth as the village of Memot, which is in Kompong Cham Province in the southeast, Saloth Sar himself has said that he was born in northern Kompong Thom Province, in the north-central part of the country. This version is accepted as correct by most authorities.

Like many Cambodians, Saloth Sar was of mixed Khmer and Chinese descent. As head of the Khmer Rouge and of Democratic Kampuchea, he was to exalt the virtues of the humble peasant class, yet his family were not peasants. They were members

His record suggests that Sar was a striving, ambitious young man who at an early age decided, consciously or not, to play a greater role in his country's life than his farming father had.
—ELIZABETH BECKER
American journalist, on the young Saloth Sar

Ieng Sary, Pol Pot's close adviser and deputy, with the Khmer Rouge in the jungles of Cambodia in the 1970s. Pol Pot almost never appeared in public, before journalists, or in talks with anyone from outside the Khmer Rouge leadership; such appearances were left to Ieng Sary and a handful of others in Pol Pot's inner circle.

of the rural village aristocracy, moderately prosperous farmers who owned their own land, unlike the many poorer folk who worked as hired labor on large plantations and estates. According to Haing Ngor, a Cambodian doctor who has recounted his suffering under Pol Pot's regime in a book entitled *A Cambodian Odyssey*, Saloth Sar's family boasted several connections to the royal household in Phnom Penh. One of his aunts was a concubine, or royal mistress, in the harem of King Monivong, who was Sihanouk's uncle and predecessor on the throne; it is also said that a cousin of the family occupied the favored post of first-ranking harem wife, or secondary wife to the king.

Perhaps through these royal connections, Saloth Sar's older brother, whose name was Loth Suong, was able to obtain a position in the palace's protocol office, which regulated official ceremonies. The position was neither important nor influential, but it guaranteed a government salary and carried with it a certain prestige. It also gave Saloth Sar's family a footing in Phnom Penh. When Saloth Sar was five years old, he was sent there to be raised by his brother and to receive an education.

For 6 years, until he was 11, Saloth Sar lived and studied in Phnom Penh. Accounts of this period differ in their details. Pol Pot once claimed that he had spent the entire six years living and studying in a pagoda school (a school attached to a Buddhist temple). According to other sources, he lived for most of this time with his brother, although he did study at the temple school for six years; these other sources say he also visited the palace often with his brother and learned to speak the special form of very polite, elaborate Khmer that was sometimes called "the royal language." If he did not live in the temple school for the six-year period, however, it is certain that he lived there for at least several months, possibly a year. It was customary throughout Cambodia for boys to spend as much as a year living in a temple or monastery, studying and serving the monks, even if they had no intention of devoting themselves to a religious life.

Saloth Sar was not an inspired student. At the end of the six years, he was required to take an

> *Unfortunately Pol Pot the maker of policy was the same as Saloth Sar the mediocre student. . . . It was senseless to build huge canal systems and dams without using engineers, but then Pol Pot was like that. He tried to make reality fit politics instead of the other way around.*
>
> —HAING NGOR
> Cambodian refugee

King Sisowath Monivong, Sihanouk's uncle, during his coronation ceremonies in Phnom Penh in 1928. An aunt of Saloth Sar's (Pol Pot's real name) was one of Monivong's concubines; through this royal connection Saloth Sar's family was able to send him to the capital for an education.

examination to certify that he had completed elementary school. He failed and was therefore unable to enroll in any of the city's well-regarded secondary schools, so he returned to his family's home in the country. From there he was sent to a secondary school in Kompong Cham Province. It was there that he spent 1941, a year that marked several important events in Cambodian history.

King Monivong died in early 1941, and the French were required to name a successor to the throne. Many Cambodians expected Prince Monireth, Monivong's son, to be the next king. But the French authorities, feeling that Monireth was too interested in independence and might be difficult to control, surprised everyone by selecting Prince Sihanouk, who was crowned on April 25. He was 18 years old.

Outside events also shook Cambodia in 1941. World War II was being fought on the battlefields of Europe, where France and its allies were pitted against Germany and the Axis powers. Now Japan had begun to carry the war into Asia and the Pacific. Even before the death of King Monivong, Japanese troops had invaded Cambodia and marched into Phnom Penh. The invasion was fairly peaceful, though; neither the French nor the Cambodians attempted to resist the much stronger Japanese forces, and in turn the Japanese permitted the French colonial administration to remain in charge

Part of the royal palace in Phnom Penh. According to some accounts, Saloth Sar studied at a Buddhist school from age 5 to age 11 and sometimes visited the palace with his brother, who worked in the royal protocol office.

of the country — but under Japanese military control.

The Japanese occupation of Phnom Penh had little direct effect on the day-to-day lives of many rural Cambodians, including Saloth Sar. Throughout most of the rest of World War II, Saloth Sar remained at his provincial school. But in Phnom Penh the events of the war years gave great impetus to Khmer nationalism and propelled the anti-French independence movement forward.

The first leader of the independence movement to achieve wide recognition was Son Ngoc Thanh, a Cambodian who had been born in southern Vietnam, or Kampuchea Krom. After university studies in Paris, he settled in Phnom Penh and became the secretary of the Buddhist Institute. He was one of the founders of the first Khmer-language newspaper, the *Nagaravatta*, which began publication in

1936. Son Ngoc Thanh and his associates used the newspaper and the institute to encourage discussions about colonialism and nationalism.

Another focus for the growing anti-French feeling was the Sisowath School, a highly regarded French-style academy that opened in Phnom Penh not long before the war. The children of the well-to-do, French-speaking urban elite were educated there, and the graduates formed an organization called the Friendship Association to help each other find jobs. They asked Son Ngoc Thanh, who had studied law for one year in Paris, to serve as their legal adviser. Before long, the alumni group of the Sisowath School had become a center of debate about the evils of colonialism and a source of new recruits for the anti-French movement. Son Ngoc Thanh succeeded in uniting the traditional and largely rural population of Buddhist monks with the sophisticated urban intellectuals of the capital in a single movement.

Two other anti-French movements were taking shape in other parts of the country. One was an offshoot of the Communist party that had started in northern Vietnam under the leadership of Ho Chi Minh. Ho founded the Indochinese Communist party (ICP) in 1930, the year the Buddhist Institute was established. (Indochina was a name used by the French and other foreigners for Vietnam, Cambodia, and Laos collectively.) The headquarters of

A group of Buddhist monks at prayer in Phnom Penh. During Saloth Sar's childhood, Cambodia's predominantly Buddhist society was deeply traditional and religious. Despite three decades of enormous suffering, it remains so today.

the international Communist party in Moscow gave the ICP responsibility for organizing Communist parties in Laos and Cambodia as well as Vietnam, but the ICP made almost no headway in Cambodia for a decade after its inception. Its activities were limited to a few areas along the Vietnam border.

On the other side of the country, near the Thailand border, another group was forming in opposition to the French. This was the non-Communist Khmer Issarak (Independent Khmer), which was started by Cambodians living in Thailand. While the Issarak encouraged a program of armed resistance to the French, it did not offer an organized political philosophy or program. Still, the Issarak attracted far more recruits than the ICP during the 1940s.

But in the early 1940s, the center of anticolonial activity was Phnom Penh. The Japanese occupation officials encouraged the Cambodian nationalists to oppose the French, because they hoped to eliminate all European claims to Asian territory. When Son Ngoc Thanh and his followers called openly for revolt against France, the French closed the *Nagaravatta* down. They also arrested a well-known monk named Hem Cheav, who had urged Cambodian soldiers to desert from the French colonial army. Hem Cheav became one of the earliest martyrs of Cambodia's independence movement. He and another monk were arrested by the French and sent to a prison island near Saigon. Hem Cheav died there three years later.

Hem Cheav's arrest gave Son Ngoc Thanh the occasion to organize the first independence rally. With the support of Japanese officers, he announced that on July 20, 1942, he would march on the office of the senior French administrator and present demands for Cambodian independence and the release of political prisoners such as Hem Cheav. Almost 2,000 residents of Phnom Penh answered Son Ngoc Thanh's summons to join the march. The protest was forcibly broken up by French security police, who arrested 200 of the demonstrators and drove many more out of the city. But their chief target, Son Ngoc Thanh, managed to escape. Japanese officers in Phnom Penh hid him and then

In the 1930s, Son Ngoc Thanh became the leader of Cambodia's first independence movement. He would play an important role in the nation's politics for the next 40 years.

smuggled him to Tokyo, where he stayed for several years. He became an enthusiastic supporter of the Japanese war effort throughout Asia.

The independence movement in Phnom Penh appeared to have suffered a severe setback. Its leaders were dispersed: Hem Cheav was in prison in Vietnam, and Son Ngoc Thanh was in hiding in Japan. But in 1943, Japan began to set up new regimes — superficially independent but in reality answerable to Tokyo — in many of the European colonies that it had occupied, including Burma, Java, and Singapore. By this time the Pacific war had begun to go badly for the Japanese. Fearful of defeat, they could no longer collaborate with the colonial administrations of the European powers; they now wanted to turn the colonies into sovereign states that would be loyal to Japan. Thanks to Japan, therefore, Cambodia was granted "independence" on March 9, 1945.

On that day, the Japanese suddenly arrested the entire French military and police force in Cambodia and interned the civilian French population. Four days later, King Sihanouk canceled the treaties his ancestors had signed with France and declared the French protectorate at an end.

Sihanouk and the Cambodians soon found that they had exchanged one bad master for another. The Japanese requisitioned many tons of rice and at least 7,000 Cambodian men for its armies. They also failed to force Thailand to return a large piece of northwestern Cambodia that had been seized by the Thai army in 1941. (This territory, amounting to almost one-third of Cambodia's total area, was returned to Cambodia after World War II ended.) As disappointing as the new regime proved to be, however, there was nonetheless contention over who would be its leader. The Japanese brought Son Ngoc Thanh back to Cambodia and made him foreign minister under King Sihanouk, but he felt he deserved a more important position.

August 9, 1945, was an eventful day around the world. On that day the United States dropped an atomic bomb on the Japanese city of Nagasaki, thereby sealing Japan's defeat and signaling the end

It is a year during which the Empire of the Rising Sun, the liberator of the Asian people, has given to Cambodia the inestimable gift of independence.
—PRINCE NORODOM SIHANOUK
on Japan's movement to
establish a regime in
Phnom Penh, March 1945

Ho Chi Minh, president of North Vietnam. One of the key political and military figures of the mid-20th century, Ho, a Communist, successfully led the Vietnamese independence movement against France, then reunited his nation by defeating the U.S.-backed capitalist regime of South Vietnam.

of the war. And also on that day the nationalist supporters of Son Ngoc Thanh staged a coup in Phnom Penh and named him prime minister. By this time, France had told the world that it intended to reclaim the colonies it had held before the war. Desperate to stop the French advance, Son Ngoc Thanh tried to form an alliance with the Vietminh, Ho Chi Minh's Vietnamese Communist group, which was fiercely opposed to the restoration of French rule. Sihanouk feared that such an alliance would end in Vietnamese domination of Cambodia, and he sent a message to the French in Saigon, asking them to return and take control of Cambodia.

That plea was answered on October 10, 1945, when units of the British, French, and Indian armies marched into Phnom Penh. Son Ngoc Thanh was arrested for treason, and Sihanouk remained on the throne. He agreed to a renewal of French administrative control, although the language was new: Cambodia was now "an autonomous state within the French union" instead of a protectorate or a colony.

Matters did not go as smoothly for the French in Vietnam. Indeed, the end of World War II saw the beginning of a conflict in Vietnam that would have enormous consequences for Cambodia in the years to come.

During World War II, the Vietminh had sided with the Allied forces against the Japanese. At the end of the war, however, the Vietminh and the French found themselves at odds. Ho Chi Minh had declared Vietnam an independent nation in September 1945, and Bao Dai, the hereditary emperor of Vietnam, had accepted the declaration. Just a few weeks later, the French — with the assistance of their British allies — returned to reclaim their colony in Vietnam. Fighting broke out between the Vietminh, who were centered in the north, around the city of Hanoi, and the French, who were strongest in the south, around Saigon. The fighting would continue until 1954.

In Cambodia, meanwhile, the French had agreed to allow the formation of political parties and elections for a national assembly in 1946. The Democratic party, which was headed by a thoughtful and moderate member of the royal family named Prince

French troops in Saigon, Vietnam, prepare to go into action against Ho Chi Minh's Vietminh rebels in the early 1950s. The guerrilla war in French Indochina sapped France's strength and stepped up Southeast Asian demands for independence.

Youthevong, attracted most of the nationalists, including the intellectual group at the Sisowath School, Son Ngoc Thanh's followers, the Buddhist Institute group, and such Cambodians as had democratic or socialist ideas. In the election, this party won control of the new assembly and called for immediate and complete independence from France. The assembly, however, had only an "advisory" role and no legislative power. It is nevertheless possible that the popular and capable Democratic party might have achieved some of its goals had not Youthevong died in 1947. At that time, the Democratic party ceased to be a significant force in Cambodian politics.

While all of these events were taking place, Saloth Sar had managed to pass his courses and was graduated from school in 1944, at the age of 19. He thereupon left Kompong Cham for Phnom Penh and enrolled in a technical school to study carpentry. Once again he was under the guardianship of his brother Loth Suong. Many years later, Loth Suong recalled that at this time Saloth Sar was kind, pleas-

Ieng Sary at the United Nations in 1978. He met Saloth Sar when both were teenage students at a Phnom Penh technical school.

ant, studious, and unremarkable, not at all political and certainly not a troublemaker. But it was during this period that Saloth Sar met and became associated with a group of political activists, some of whom were certainly regarded as troublemakers by the French.

These were the young intellectuals and nationalists who formed the core of the Sisowath School group. Although most members of the group were graduates of the prestigious Sisowath School, some students from the technical schools also joined their movement. Saloth Sar was one such technical student. He hung around the Sisowath School and took part in long, passionate political discussions in its colonnaded courtyard and at the long tables of its dining hall. He became friendly with one of the Sisowath student leaders, an intelligent and affable young man named Ieng Sary.

Like Son Ngoc Thanh, Ieng Sary was a Khmer Krom, a Cambodian from southern Vietnam. (He had changed his name from Kim Trang in order to sound more like a Khmer.) He was a brilliant student, especially in mathematics, and earned a scholarship to Sisowath. A fervent nationalist, he organized in 1946 a student group called Liberation of Cambodia from French Colonialism. As head of this movement, Ieng Sary led the first student protests in the country's history, and he also tried to organize a national strike to protest Sihanouk's rejection of the Democratic party's call for independence.

All in all, Ieng Sary was a spirited and stimulating comrade. He was one of Saloth Sar's closest associates for nearly half a century after their days at the Sisowath School. He would one day be Saloth Sar's right-hand man in the Khmer Rouge and in Democratic Kampuchea.

But now, however, both young men sought to complete their education. Through bribery or political influence, they managed to obtain two of the rare scholarships to study in Paris. Ironically, these scholarships were paid for by Sihanouk and the French, whom Saloth Sar and Ieng Sary would come back from Paris determined to destroy.

> *I will die happy if I were sure that my country will be liberated from the foreign yoke. I pray for freedom.*
> —HEM CHEAV
> Cambodian monk, uttering his last words, in a French prison near Saigon

4

The Paris Cell

Saloth Sar arrived in Paris in 1949, at the age of 21, and enrolled at a technical school called the École Française de Radio-éléctricité, where he was to study radio electronics. It was his first trip outside Cambodia, but in his extremely rare interviews and in his writings he has said nothing about his impressions of Paris or the experience of visiting Europe. Almost as soon as he arrived, he was absorbed into a group of Cambodian students and intellectuals who were living in Paris. Ieng Sary arrived in Paris in 1950, quickly renewing his friendship with Saloth Sar and becoming acquainted with the other Cambodian students. Over the next few years, this circle was the nucleus of what would eventually become the Khmer Rouge.

Among the leading figures in the Cambodian student community in Paris were three brothers, Thiounn Mumm, Thiounn Prasith, and Thiounn Thioenn. They belonged to a wealthy and aristocratic family and were considerably more sophisticated than either Saloth Sar or Ieng Sary. Yet they befriended both men as well as many other Cam-

They arrived in Paris when the political climate was vibrant and French intellectuals were shaping the themes that dominated postwar attitudes. . . . Their transformation from strident democrats to militant Marxists was facilitated by the French communists. . . .
—ELIZABETH BECKER
American journalist, on Saloth Sar and Ieng Sary's stay in Paris

A French Communist party demonstration in Paris in the late 1940s. Saloth Sar, Ieng Sary, and a core of other young Cambodian intellectuals came under the influence of Communist ideology as students in Paris during this period.

bodian students from humble backgrounds, and in the years to come they supported and were spokesmen for Cambodia's nationalist and Communist movements.

In the 1940s and 1950s, Paris had a lively political climate that excited and inspired the colonial students. The French Communist party (PCF) was large and vigorous, embracing both intellectuals and workers. The strong anticolonial position of the French Communists appealed to the young Cambodian nationalists, who also approved of the increasingly anti-American stance of the PCF. Few, if any, members of Saloth Sar's circle had seriously considered adopting communism before arriving in France; they had left communism to the Vietminh in the border jungles and had merely called for the end of the monarchy and the establishment of a self-governing republic. Their contacts with teachers and writers in the PCF, however, soon convinced them that communism was a powerful weapon against French colonialism — after all, it seemed to be working for Ho Chi Minh in northern Vietnam. The Cambodians declared themselves willing and eager to learn more, and Maurice Thorez, the secretary-general of the PCF, helped them form a Communist study group.

The center of the group's activities was an apartment at 28, rue St. André des Arts, in the Latin Quarter, the district of the city that contains the University of Paris and has been the haunt of students and intellectuals since medieval times. Ieng Sary, Thiounn Mumm, Thiounn Prasith, and another Cambodian student named Ok Sakun lived in

The exterior of the French electronics school attended by Saloth Sar beginning in 1949; he was joined by Ieng Sary the following year. Both were sent to Paris on scholarships sponsored by Sihanouk and the Cambodian government.

this apartment, and the other members of the study group — among them Saloth Sar — spent long hours there in reading and discussion.

One memorable event of the Paris years was the wedding of Ieng Sary. Shortly before leaving Phnom Penh, he had become engaged to a young woman named Khieu Tirith, the daughter of a judge. Attractive and popular, she was one of the first women to study at the Sisowath School, where she received excellent grades and became devoted to the cause of Cambodian nationalism. Although her social status was superior to Ieng Sary's, she had fallen in love with him — partly, as she said years later, because she believed that he was a natural leader who would do much for Cambodia.

Khieu Tirith came to Paris to study English literature at the Sorbonne, one of the colleges of the University of Paris. Upon her arrival, she and Ieng Sary were married in a gala celebration. They rented a ballroom and invited everyone they knew in Paris. The guests included the official Cambodian representative to France and his wife; other members of Phnom Penh's upper middle class who happened to be in France on business; Marxists and members of the PCF; and students from Cambodia, Vietnam, Algeria, Tunisia, and Morocco. "There were no divisions then among the Cambodians," Khieu Tirith later recalled. "We were all united." The guests chipped in 200 francs each to pay for the party, and Thiounn Prasith, a talented chef, prepared the food. The wedding was an unusually festive occasion in the lives of Saloth Sar, Ieng Sary, and their friends, who were generally rather earnest. It is also notable because it introduced Saloth Sar to Khieu Tirith's older sister, Khieu Ponnary.

Ponnary had accompanied Khieu Tirith to Paris in order to study for a teacher's certificate. She was less striking in appearance and less outgoing than her sister Tirith, but she was a fine student and a serious thinker. At Tirith's urging, she began attending the Communist study sessions. There is no evidence to suggest that Ponnary was as deeply committed to political causes as Tirith was or that she and Saloth Sar fell passionately in love. But Ponnary did ally herself with the nationalist-Communist movement that was being shaped by Ieng Sary and Saloth Sar, and she and Saloth Sar became engaged.

The Paris years were crucial to Saloth Sar's political development and eventual emergence as a dedicated, hard-line Communist. One important formative experience took place in 1950, when he traveled to Yugoslavia, which was then in the process of establishing itself as an independent Communist nation under the leadership of Marshal Tito. Saloth Sar spent a month working in a youth brigade that was building a highway from the city of Zagreb to the capital, Belgrade. He admired Yugoslavia for attempting to follow what Tito called "the independent road to socialism" while remaining free of domination from the Soviet Union and other powerful Communist nations. He felt that it might be possible to steer Cambodia down a similar road.

In the early 1950s, Saloth Sar emerged as a leader among the Cambodian nationalists in Paris. He was one of the contributors to an anti-Sihanouk publication called *Cambodian Student*. Like everyone who wrote for the paper, he used a pen name to conceal his identity so that his government scholarship would not be withdrawn for antigovernment activities. The pen name he selected was "Original Khmer." It is the first known pseudonym of the man who would later call himself Pol Pot, and it reflects an important facet of his character: his extreme pride in the Khmer ethnic heritage. By the time he came to power in Democratic Kampuchea in the 1970s, that pride had been transformed into a violent fear and hatred of other ethnic and racial groups.

"Monarchy or Democracy?" was the title of an article by Saloth Sar that appeared in *Cambodian Student* in 1952. In it, he attacked not just the French colonialists but also Sihanouk, who had collaborated with the French to restore the colonial government. This, he said, made the king an enemy of the Cambodian people. A democracy that incorporated Communist economic and social principles, he wrote, would be the most modern, humane, and

Finally, the politics of the king will provoke a civil war that will burn everything—even the pagodas. The monks, the people, the bureaucrats will experience the sadness of the families, the women and children will be smashed by tanks, burned by napalm; the harvest will be destroyed.

—POL POT
writing as "Original Khmer" in 1952

effective form of government for Cambodia. The country's only hope for the future was the abolition of the monarchy.

Original Khmer ended his article with a prediction that Sihanouk would soon manage to obtain independence for Cambodia from France. Because of this, he said, the king would be hailed as the father of Cambodian independence, even though he had been as firmly opposed as the French to Son Ngoc Thanh, Hem Cheav, and the student nationalist movement. After independence, Saloth Sar warned, Sihanouk's power would be stronger than ever, and he would "shut up the people, expel those who oppose the policies of the king." The prediction was an accurate one. Through an international campaign of political lobbying and publicizing his nation's cause, an effort he called "the king's crusade," Sihanouk succeeded in obtaining independence for Cambodia at the end of 1953. By that time, Saloth Sar had returned to Cambodia.

He was the first of the Paris circle to return to the kingdom. He did so because his scholarship was

A view of Belgrade, Yugoslavia, in 1950, when Saloth Sar spent a year in the Communist country to participate in road-building work. It was around this time that Ieng Sary married a Cambodian, Khieu Tirith; her sister, Khieu Ponnary, would later become Saloth Sar's wife.

Independence Plaza in Phnom Penh, built to mark Cambodia's independence from France, which was granted at the end of 1953. Cambodian autonomy was won mainly through the efforts of Sihanouk, whose public crusade brought his nation's plight to world attention.

withdrawn — officially because he had failed all three of the required examinations at the radio-electronics school but possibly also because he was now known to the government as a political agitator. Ieng Sary and Khieu Tirith remained in Paris, living on money sent from Cambodia by her mother; she continued her studies at the Sorbonne, but Ieng Sary dropped out of school and devoted himself full-time to politics. Also remaining in Paris was Thiounn Mumm, who served as a sort of elder brother and adviser to the next group of Cambodian students to join the study group. Among them were Khieu Samphan, Son Sen, and Hou Youn, three future leaders of the Khmer Rouge.

Saloth Sar arrived in Phnom Penh in January 1953, and he and Khieu Ponnary were married soon thereafter. At about this time, Saloth Sar visited his

brother Loth Suong, who had served as his guardian in Phnom Penh during his student days. Loth Suong listened to Saloth Sar's enthusiastic accounts of Yugoslavian road work and French communism and marveled at the change in his brother, whom he had never suspected of having political interests.

The newly returned Saloth Sar was most eager to get involved in Cambodian politics. In Paris he had been a member of the PCF and a recognized political agitator. In Phnom Penh, however, his only political connection was with the Democratic party, which had little strength. He was not sympathetic to the Issarak movement, which called for Cambodian independence but said nothing about abolishing the monarchy. And when he sought out the Cambodian Communist movement, Saloth Sar found some surprises.

The first surprise was that there did not exist a unified, nationwide Communist party. Communism had not gotten off to a flying start in Cambodia. As early as the 1930s or 1940s, some Cambodians had joined Ho Chi Minh's ICP and allied themselves with the Vietminh, or Vietnamese Communists, but in view of the long-standing antagonism between the Khmer and the Vietnamese peoples, many were reluctant to join a movement that was dominated by Vietnam.

The movement took a step forward in 1950, when Cambodian Communists held the First National Congress of Khmer Resistance on April 17 and adopted the name United Issarak Front (UIF). They were led by a former monk named Achr Mean. He had joined the ICP in 1946 and adopted the name Son Ngoc Minh (a nom de guerre that referred to the Cambodian nationalist leader Son Ngoc Thanh and to the Vietminh). Son Ngoc Minh advised the Cambodian Communists to use the name "Issarak" in the hope of attracting peasants who might confuse it with the non-Communist Khmer Issarak. Australian scholar Ben Kiernan, who has written extensively about modern Cambodian history, quotes one Communist who recalled of those early days, "It was difficult to know who were the real

Issaraks, the loyal revolutionaries, and who were the bandits and robbers."

In 1951, the UIF formed its own political party, which it called the Khmer People's Revolutionary party (KPRP). But the KPRP was not able to obtain recognition from Moscow as an independent Communist party until 1960. Between 1951 and 1960, members of the KPRP also had to join the ICP, which was the only Communist party in Cambodia that was recognized by the international Communist community during that nine-year period. The two groups were frequently at odds and seldom cooperated; after 1960, when the official history of the Communist party in Cambodia was written and rewritten several times, a great rift developed between those who felt that the party had gotten its start in 1951 with the help of the Vietnamese and those who claimed that it began independently in 1960. Furthermore, both groups were strongest in isolated sections of the countryside, and neither had much of a presence in the capital.

In 1953, however, Saloth Sar simply wanted to become part of the Communist movement. One of his brothers introduced him to someone in the ICP, and Saloth Sar transferred his membership in the PCF to the ICP. Like many Communist parties — and other underground groups as well — the ICP was organized into small units called cells. The members of each cell knew each other, but each of them was supposed to know only one party member outside the cell. The idea behind the cell organization is that it should prevent any one member from identifying or implicating more than a handful of other members. In practice, party members such as Saloth Sar often become acquainted with a great many members outside their cells, but the cell functions as the basic unit of communication and organization within the party.

Life within the party proved to be another surprise for Saloth Sar. He was assigned to a cell in a rural area outside Phnom Penh. The cell consisted of 10 Vietnamese and 10 Cambodians. To his dismay, he found that the Vietnamese Communists clearly felt superior to the Cambodians. The Cambodians were

expected to do menial chores in party compounds and to listen respectfully to the wisdom of the Vietnamese. Saloth Sar was put to work scrubbing kitchens and emptying latrines — hardly the dynamic role he had envisioned for himself as the Original Khmer.

Khieu Tirith, his sister-in-law, recalled it as "a very sad experience. The Vietminh put all the students from Paris in the background. They gave them kitchen chores, to carry excrement. Saloth Sar had to carry excrement for the Vietnamese. There was no political work." Saloth Sar resented this treatment, which reinforced what appears to have been a basic dislike and distrust of the Vietnamese. From the beginning, he felt that Cambodian communism should be entirely in Cambodian hands.

In the meantime, Cambodia gained its independence from France, and as Original Khmer had predicted, Sihanouk was regarded around the world and by most of his countrymen as the father of Cambodian independence. The Issarak movement — the non-Communist freedom fighters — lost most of its members, although a few of them joined the Communists. Then, in early 1954, the Vietminh de-

French prisoners after the decisive Battle of Dien Bien Phu in 1954. The Vietminh victory in the battle forced France to end its war against Ho Chi Minh's rebels and meet them instead at the negotiating table.

French premier Pierre Mendès-France and Chinese premier Zhou Enlai at the Geneva Conference in May 1954. Accords signed at the talks led to the creation of two independent nations, Communist North Vietnam and capitalist South Vietnam, and to the recognition of Sihanouk's government in Cambodia; the Cambodian Communists, however, were not recognized.

feated the French army at Dien Bien Phu in Vietnam. The French, who had been fighting the Vietnamese Communists since 1946, finally acknowledged defeat. They agreed to discuss peace terms with the Vietminh in Geneva, Switzerland, in May 1954.

That conference set the stage for a new war in Vietnam. The conference was attended by delegations from France, Great Britain, the United States, the Soviet Union, China, Vietnam, Laos, and Cambodia. The French and the Vietminh agreed to a "temporary" division of Vietnam into North Vietnam, which would be governed by the Communists from Hanoi, and South Vietnam, which would have a non-Communist government backed by France and the United States. It was agreed that nationwide elections would be held to unify the country under a single government, but South Vietnam refused to hold these elections, and the country remained divided for more than two decades.

As for Cambodia, the Geneva Conference established it as a sovereign nation, with King Sihanouk as head of state. The conference gave no recognition at all to the Cambodian Communists, although in both Laos and Vietnam the Communist parties were granted territory and political rights.

Saloth Sar and many other Cambodian Communists felt that their Communist brethren in the Soviet Union, China, and North Vietnam had betrayed them at Geneva by not insisting on recognition of the KPRP, the UIF, or the ICP in Cambodia. When Sihanouk returned triumphantly to Phnom Penh from the conference, the country's Communists realized that they had two choices: They could try to keep the movement alive in Cambodia, against what looked certain to be powerful opposition from Sihanouk, or they could go into exile in North Vietnam and wait for a better opportunity to strike against the king.

About 1,000 Communists, including Son Ngoc Minh, chose the latter alternative. Disguised in Vietnamese uniforms, they crossed into North Vietnam and dispersed among the Vietminh forces. One of these Cambodian Communists, a man named Ieng Lim, later explained that the Vietnamese had invited him to come to North Vietnam for "an education." He accepted with pleasure, expecting to be gone for two years or so. He was not able to return for 16 years. Cambodians like Ieng Lim were scattered across North Vietnam. Years later, when these Cambodians returned from North Vietnam to join the Khmer Rouge, they were treated with scorn by their fellow Communists for having fled to safety while their comrades fought to keep the revolution alive at home.

Among the Communists who remained in Cambodia, however, was Saloth Sar. He was about to witness a decade in which Cambodian communism would have to struggle for its existence. It would also be a period that would see the birth of the Khmer Rouge.

The Cambodians, they have two faces, two aspects. They can smile, and they can kill.
—PRINCE NORODOM SIHANOUK
Cambodian ruler

5

Brother Number One

Cambodia received its independence in 1953. In 1954, the Geneva Conference divided Vietnam, and the Vietminh and many of their Cambodian comrades withdrew into North Vietnam. At this point, the Communists in Phnom Penh took stock of their situation. They numbered fewer than 60: about 40 members of the ICP, 10 or so intellectuals who had joined the PCF in Paris, and a handful from the Thai Communist party.

Their nominal leader was Son Ngoc Minh, but he was in North Vietnam and out of touch, so the real leader of the Cambodian Communists was Minh's second-in-command, Sieu Heng. Sieu Heng was put in charge of recruiting party members and organizing cells in the countryside. The third-ranking Communist, Tou Samouth, was put in charge of the movement in all the cities and towns. At this time, Saloth Sar was nothing more than a low-ranking cadre, as fully initiated party members were called.

Independence, national sovereignty, self-reliance . . . and revolutionary violence.
—party line espoused by Cambodian Communists in the early 1960s

Khmer Rouge rebels in southwestern Cambodia in the early 1970s. Saloth Sar and his fellow Communists went underground in 1962 and retreated into the bush, where the organization evolved into a tough, lean, and ruthless guerrilla army.

The Phnom Penh Communists had a three-part plan. First, they set up an openly Communist political party called the Pracheachon (People's party) to compete in the elections that were scheduled for 1955. Second, certain party members were told to obtain positions within Sihanouk's government, keeping their Communist affiliations secret. Third, many cadres were given the assignment of finding jobs as teachers, writers, and journalists — again, keeping their membership in the Communist party secret — while carefully recruiting new members from among the city's students, workers, and intellectuals. Saloth Sar belonged to this third group.

The Communists were determined to oust King Sihanouk, but he was a wily opponent. As Haing Ngor puts it in *A Cambodian Odyssey*: "Sihanouk outmaneuvered them at every turn." The king soon realized that although he had obtained independence for Cambodia, he could not return the country to the absolute monarchical rule of precolonial times. Sihanouk carried out a masterstroke of strategy in 1955. He stepped down from the throne and gave up the kingship so that he could run for elected office. His father, Suramarit, became a figurehead king; when King Suramarit died five years later, the kingship remained vacant. Sihanouk, who retained the title of prince after leaving the throne, formed his own political party to compete in the 1955 elections. He called it the Sangkum Reastr Niyum, which means "People's Socialist Community," but the emphasis in the Sangkum's political platform was on loyalty to Sihanouk, not on socialism.

The elections were a great success for the Sangkum. Three of the Pracheachon candidates were arrested and jailed shortly before voting day, and some members of the Pracheachon fled to the countryside in fear of harassment by Sihanouk's police. One candidate was Thiounn Mumm, who had returned to Cambodia to run for office. Mumm felt so threatened during the campaign that he went back to France and stayed there for 16 years. When the votes were counted, Sihanouk had been elected prime minister, and the Sangkum had won every seat in the National Assembly. As American journalist Eliz-

abeth Becker points out in *When the War Was Over*, a history of the Khmer Rouge, "The Pracheachon's greatest accomplishment was to fill the police dossiers with the names of all the leftists who had exposed themselves in the election."

As prime minister, Sihanouk used a number of methods to discourage and repress the Communist movement, partly because he did not want any group to threaten his own power and partly because he feared that the Vietnamese influence on the Communists would lead to Vietnamese domination over Cambodia. His attack on the Communist movement took place on several levels.

With the intention of limiting their ability to criticize or oppose his government, Sihanouk appointed several of the more moderate leading leftists to his cabinet. Among these were Hou Youn and

Sihanouk addresses a rally in 1955, the year he gave up his title as king to compete in Cambodia's first elections. Nevertheless, traditional Cambodians still looked upon Prince Sihanouk, as he has been called ever since, as a semidivine figure.

Khieu Samphan, who had been members of the Communist study group in the rue St. André des Arts in Paris.

Khieu Samphan was widely respected by Communists and non-Communists alike for his personal integrity and his modest life-style, which was conspicuous in the midst of the corruption and ostentation that flourished in government circles. He was the editor of *L'Observateur*, a French-language newspaper that promoted Communist views and frequently criticized the government. Sihanouk at first had Khieu Samphan harassed by the police and even jailed him; then, when Khieu Samphan's popularity continued to grow, Sihanouk made him his secretary of state for commerce. Together with the existence of the Pracheachon, Khieu Samphan's presence in the cabinet made it look as if Sihanouk were tolerant of the Communists.

On a less public level, however, Sihanouk carried out a policy that the Communists referred to as "the war in the shadows." He persecuted journalists and newspaper editors who published material that he deemed seditious, or damaging to the government. One of Saloth Sar's brothers was a victim of this policy; he was jailed briefly for writing an article that criticized Sihanouk's acceptance of American military aid. In this shadow war, Communists were jailed without charges or intimidated into leaving Phnom Penh. Some were killed. Sihanouk also had a hidden weapon: Sieu Heng, the leader of the Cam-

The 19th-century German political philosopher Karl Marx provided the basis for the international socialist and communist movements of the 20th century. In 1960 the various factions among Cambodian Communists united to form a single party independent of the Vietnamese Communists.

bodian Communists, who was secretly working for Sihanouk. He supplied the prime minister with the Communists' names and information about their activities. When Sieu Heng openly rallied to Sihanouk's side in 1959, the Communists looked foolish and felt deeply betrayed. Sieu Heng's defection contributed to the mood of suspicion and mutual distrust that remained with the Khmer Rouge throughout their years in power.

The Cambodian Communists faced a further difficulty at this time. As the leader of independent Cambodia, Sihanouk pursued a course of international neutrality. In the face of unremitting pressure from the United States, he refused to sign treaties that would make Cambodia a U.S. ally. Cambodia remained a nonaligned nation — that is, it was neither part of the Communist bloc nor allied with the United States and its partners. Moreover, just as it received U.S. aid, Sihanouk's Cambodia also enjoyed cordial relations with the major Communist nations and obtained financial aid from both China and the Soviet Union.

But these Communist superpowers more or less ignored the Cambodian ICP and the Pracheachon. As a result, the Cambodian Communists felt that they were forced to go it alone in these years. They felt betrayed by and resentful of the international Communist parties, and although they later accepted considerable aid from China, they insisted on retaining their autonomy. The fiercely self-reliant pride of the Khmer Rouge, which was later reflected in the xenophobic and isolationist policies of Democratic Kampuchea, had its roots in this period.

While these events were unfolding, Saloth Sar pursued the path that had been set for him by the party. He obtained a job as a teacher at a new private high school called Kampuchea But (Child of Cambodia). The school was run by leftists and Communists, but their political activity at the school was very low-key. Kampuchea But soon gained a reputation as a school with high academic standards. After he returned to Phnom Penh in 1957, Ieng Sary got a job teaching there, too.

The wives of the two men, Khieu Ponnary and Khieu Tirith, taught at government schools. Under Sihanouk, the number of schools in the country increased greatly, and student enrollments rose to the highest point they had yet reached. People like the sisters Khieu Tirith and Khieu Ponnary, who were extensively educated and had studied in Europe, had no difficulty finding teaching jobs. In fact, Tirith was offered a good position in Sihanouk's government, but — on the orders of the Communist party — she turned it down. Instead, again at the party's request, she worked extra hours at her school. "I could work as many extra hours as I wanted," she later recalled, "so I earned much money — so much money I could have built a villa or bought a car, but I didn't." The extra money went instead to finance Communist party activities. Both Tirith and Ponnary contributed substantial percentages of their salaries to *L'Observateur*, Khieu Samphan's newspaper.

Just as Sihanouk waged a secret "war in the shadows" against the Communists, Communists such as Saloth Sar carried on a number of clandestine activities. By day they were teachers or office workers; by night they held secret meetings, trying to recruit members, organize factory workers into collectives, and inspire strikes. Saloth Sar had become an effective speaker and organizer and was well respected within the party for his firm ideas and his unwavering commitment to communism. In 1958, when Keo Meas, the party leader in Phnom Penh under Tou Samouth, fled to North Vietnam to avoid arrest, Saloth Sar was chosen as his successor. At about this time Saloth Sar started using another pseudonym within the party: He called himself Brother Number One.

A turning point for Saloth Sar and the Communist movement came in September 1960. In the face of increased repression from Sihanouk, the leaders of the movement decided to hold a congress and found a new party with no ties to the PCF, the Vietnamese, or the old ICP. They wanted to bring together representatives from the rural and the urban cells, to write a formal party constitution based on

the ideas of Karl Marx, V. I. Lenin, and Mao Zedong, and to consolidate all of the country's Communists into a single well-organized party.

The First Party Congress consisted of 21 representatives from around the country who met for three days and nights in some abandoned train cars that were being stored in a Phnom Penh railroad station. The congress chose the name Workers' Party of Kampuchea; in 1966, this was changed to the Communist Party of Kampuchea (CPK). It also identified its ideals as "independence, national sovereignty and self-reliance, and revolutionary violence." Finally, the new party elected its central committee, the core of its leadership. Tou Samouth was chosen first, but Saloth Sar and Ieng Sary were also selected. Brother Number One was now a member of the inner circle of a brand-new and determined Communist party.

A peasant in Khmer Rouge territory in the early 1970s. Soon after Saloth Sar, then known as Brother Number One, was chosen to head the Cambodian Communists, a government crackdown forced them out of the capital and into the jungles. There Saloth Sar established the guerrilla bases from which the Khmer Rouge would fight the government for more than a decade.

Although the party roll grew slowly, Brother Number One was credited with helping to recruit a number of new members. One of them was a young man named Bu Phat. His story is told in Becker's *When the War Was Over*, and it sheds light on how the party operated.

Bu Phat was born in 1938 to a farming family in Takeo Province, in the southwestern corner of Cambodia. He earned a degree from a provincial Buddhist school and at age 17 came to Phnom Penh to study for an advanced degree. There he enrolled at Kampuchea But, where he made new friends who invited him to their homes for meals, games, and conversation. At one friend's home Bu Phat met several well-educated, cosmopolitan young men who, he discovered, were writers and editors for the *Pracheachon*, the Communist party's Khmer-language newspaper. He was touched and impressed by the "esteem" and "closeness" they shared with him, and within a year he had joined the staff of the paper. He later worked on *L'Observateur* and slept in its offices at night.

According to an autobiography that he wrote in 1978, Bu Phat did not at first know that his leftist friends belonged to an organized Communist party. They called their group Angka. (*Angka*, or *angkar*, is a Cambodian word that means "the organization," or "the system"; this is the term the Khmer Rouge always used to refer to the CPK.) It was not until 1962 — after Bu Phat had been working on the Communist newspapers for several years, had been briefly jailed at least twice, and had spent several long periods in hiding to escape arrest — that one of his contacts in Angka came to his hiding place and asked, "Well, comrade, would you like to join the party?" He formally joined the party in April, with two members of his cell as sponsors. A few months later, Bu Phat attended a study course taught by Brother Number One. "As far as I can remember," he wrote, "there were only a few disciples."

Angka moved Bu Phat to another secret hideout, and a party member visited him often "so that I would not get fed up with secretly hiding out," he said. He was told that he would soon be given an important mission in the countryside. One evening he was told to go to a large temple in the city and wait for a car with a certain license number, which he was required to memorize. He did so, and the car appeared. "I opened the door of the car to get in and it was Brother Number One," wrote Bu Phat. "He drove me once around Phnom Penh while simultaneously asking me whether I was absolutely sure I wanted to go or not."

Bu Phat assured Brother Number One of his eagerness to undertake Angka's mission. The young man was then turned over to Brother Number Two, as Ieng Sary called himself, who sent him across the border into South Vietnam. There he worked with the Vietcong, the underground Communist guerrilla army, doing propaganda radio broadcasts in the Khmer language. From there he returned to Cambodia and joined Brother Number One and other leaders of Angka as the Khmer Rouge army took shape in the late 1960s.

The story of Bu Phat's recruitment into the CPK reveals the attraction that the movement held for bright, idealistic young men who were frustrated with the stagnant, repressive politics of the Sihanouk regime. It also points up the care with which the party wrapped itself in secrecy and precaution.

But Bu Phat's story is particularly poignant because of what happened to him in his career with the Khmer Rouge. Upon his return from South Vietnam, he became one of Saloth Sar's lieutenants and an officer in the Khmer Rouge. He remained in Saloth Sar's service, rising through the Khmer Rouge ranks during years of jungle fighting. After the Khmer Rouge seized Phnom Penh and established Democratic Kampuchea in 1975, Bu Phat was made secretary of an entire sector of the country — an important post in the new bureaucracy. He was then ordered by Angka to become an official executioner, and he did so. Then, in 1978, someone within Angka accused him of treason without giving any grounds for the accusation. Bu Phat was thrown into prison, interrogated and tortured, and finally executed. Following Angka's orders faithfully to the end, he wrote out his autobiography at the instruc-

Pol Pot is mad, you know, like Hitler. Like Hitler, Pol Pot does not believe in God, but he thinks that Heaven, destiny, wants him to guide Cambodia in the way he thinks is the best for Cambodia—that is to say, the worst.
—PRINCE NORODOM SIHANOUK
Cambodian ruler

tion of his torturers. His experience in Democratic Kampuchea is a perfect example of how Pol Pot's revolution degenerated into a cycle of self-destructive violence.

In 1962, when Bu Phat first joined the CPK, Pol Pot was still Saloth Sar, Brother Number One, and the revolutionary movement was still in an embryonic stage. In the following year the ambitious Saloth Sar was elevated to a higher position in the party. It happened when Tou Samouth, the party leader, disappeared mysteriously; his fate is still unknown, but the CPK assumed that he had been assassinated by Sihanouk's police. A special party congress was held to elect his replacement, and the representatives chose Brother Number One; Ieng Sary, his inseparable companion, was also moved to a higher-ranking post. Ten years after returning from Paris, Saloth Sar was in control of the Communist party throughout the entire country.

Not long after the special congress that made Saloth Sar party secretary, student riots broke out in

The Khmer Rouge guerrilla army, which often included women, drew most of its fighters from the peasants of the Cambodian countryside. As the war in neighboring Vietnam escalated throughout the 1960s, the Khmer Rouge gained strength.

the northwestern province of Siem Reap. They were sparked not by Communist cadres but by high school students protesting the corruption and brutality of the police under Sihanouk. The students marched in the streets and burned pictures of the prince. In the ensuing riot, a policeman and several students were killed. Nothing like this had ever happened in Cambodia before. Sihanouk was furious. He demanded the resignation of all of his cabinet ministers, and he cracked down at once on the Communists in Phnom Penh, whom he blamed — quite wrongly, as it happened—for inciting the riots.

Suddenly the capital became too dangerous a place for Saloth Sar and Ieng Sary. Along with about 90 percent of the party's central committee, they slipped out of the city and melted into the jungle near the Vietnam border.

Saloth Sar and his colleagues established bases either in remote villages or in camps that they hacked out of the forest. They tended to move from base to base frequently. In order to win allies among the peasant farmers and country dwellers, Saloth Sar imposed a strict code of behavior on his followers: Theft, rape, and dishonesty were forbidden on pain of dire punishment. The peasants soon learned that members of Angka not only followed this code but also helped in the fields and sometimes contributed medicine or books to villages. For the most part, the country people tolerated Angka, and after a time some of them openly supported it. Young men and a few young women made their way to the camps to join up.

Around this time, Sihanouk coined a name for the Cambodian Communists. He called them the Khmer Rouge. (*Rouge* is French for "red," which is the symbolic color of the international Communist movement.) Although the prince used Khmer Rouge as a term of disdain, Saloth Sar and the other cadres and their followers adopted it proudly. They dreamed of the day when all Cambodians would be Khmer Rouge, and they set about transforming their small force, which consisted mostly of exiled urban intellectuals and untrained peasants, into an army to be reckoned with.

> *We are surrounded by forests, which are infested with elephants, buffaloes, rhinoceros, tigers and wild boars . . . but the mosquitoes and the leeches, though less dangerous, were the most troublesome and most inveterate plagues. . . . During the rainy season you cannot be too much on your guard; going to bed or getting up, you are ever in peril of putting your hand or foot on a venomous snake.*
> —HENRI MOUHOT
> 19th-century French explorer, on the Ratanakiri region, where Pol Pot would recruit part of his revolutionary army

6

The Birth of Pol Pot

In 1964 the United States, which had already sent military advisers and massive supplies of arms to South Vietnam, began regular bombing attacks against North Vietnam. The Americans thus hoped to prop up the tottering regime in the south and hold off the onslaught of the Communist north. Full-scale U.S. involvement in the war became complete when American combat troops went into battle against Communist forces in 1965. The military conflict in Southeast Asia had now escalated out of control.

Sihanouk immediately broke off diplomatic relations with the United States and denounced U.S. interference in Asian affairs. By this time, he had come to believe that the Vietminh Communists would ultimately win control of all of Vietnam, and he wanted to be on good terms with them. He strengthened Cambodia's diplomatic relations with both China and North Vietnam, and he allowed

You met corruption at every stage of life. . . . You could bribe your way through the courts—you could bribe your way through anything. The only people you didn't bribe were the monks; you just gave them money instead.
—SOMETH MAY
Cambodian refugee,
describing Sihanouk's
Cambodia of the 1960s

Khmer Rouge soldiers roll into newly captured Phnom Penh aboard a jeep flying the Khmer Rouge flag in 1975. The capture of the capital was the culmination of a long, brutal civil war.

these nations to use Cambodian ports and roads to get supplies to the North Vietnamese army. At the same time, however, conservative and right-wing elements in Sihanouk's government felt that he was becoming too pro-Communist and urged him to maintain some degree of cooperation with the United States. Eventually, Sihanouk was to allow armed reconnaissance and bombing raids by U.S. planes against suspected Vietcong and North Vietnamese army bases inside Cambodia.

The leaders of the right-wing, pro-U.S. faction within the government were General Lon Nol, who was Sihanouk's military commander in chief, and Prince Sirik Matak, a cousin of Sihanouk's. They had an ally in the countryside in Son Ngoc Thanh, the nationalist of the 1930s and 1940s who was now the leader of an anti-Sihanouk movement called the Free Khmer, which was based in the countryside. Son Ngoc Thanh was friendly to the United States and probably received aid from the U.S. Central Intelligence Agency (CIA), as did Lon Nol.

After the United States entered the war in Vietnam, Sihanouk found it increasingly difficult to hold Cambodia on the neutral, middle-of-the-road course he had advocated for a decade. The leftists in the capital wanted the United States kept out of Cambodia and demanded that Sihanouk openly support the Vietnamese Communists; the rightists demanded closer ties with the United States, no support for the Vietnamese Communists, and a crackdown on the Khmer Rouge.

The rightist faction was the stronger, at least temporarily, as was shown in the 1966 election. Lon Nol was elected prime minister, replacing Sihanouk, and Sirik Matak won a high-ranking post also. Sihanouk remained the official head of state and retained some power. And he was still enormously popular among traditional Cambodians, who still believed that Sihanouk was a deva-raja, or divine king. Nevertheless, his control of the country was gravely threatened.

While this was going on in Phnom Penh, Saloth Sar and his comrades were building the Khmer

Rouge in the countryside. In 1965, Saloth Sar made a secret trip to Hanoi and Beijing to seek support from the leaders of the North Vietnamese and Chinese Communist parties. He was accompanied by Ieng Sary and Khieu Tirith. The visits to both capitals went smoothly, but Saloth Sar was disappointed that no public attention was paid to him in either country. The party heads, who were still publicly on favorable terms with Sihanouk, advised him to be patient; there would be plenty of support for a Communist revolution in Cambodia, he was told, once the revolutions in Vietnam and Laos had suc-

A U.S. infantryman sets fire to the thatched roof of a home in a Vietnamese village in 1965. The United States first sent combat troops to fight alongside South Vietnamese forces in 1964. But despite more than 10 years of massive military effort, the Americans and South Vietnamese were ultimately defeated by the army of North Vietnam and the Vietcong guerrillas.

ceeded. Saloth Sar and Ieng Sary returned to their hideouts feeling that once again the Cambodian Communists had gotten the short end of the stick from their comrades abroad.

In 1967, however, the Khmer Rouge received a sudden and surprising opportunity to start the revolution themselves. Ironically, that opportunity was handed to them by Lon Nol.

The basis of Cambodia's domestic income was rice — specifically, the heavy taxes paid to the government on rice that was exported. Lon Nol was aware that a considerable amount of rice was being sold to the Vietnamese on the black market; perhaps as much as two-thirds of the country's total export harvest each year was disposed of in these illegal sales, which denied a large tax revenue to the government. His cabinet instituted a new rice collection system called *ramassage du paddy*. (*Ramassage* is French for "collection," and paddies are the diked fields used in rice cultivation.) Under the ramassage system, peasants who stockpiled rice to sell on the black market could be forced — at gunpoint by the military, if necessary — to sell their rice to govern-

A 1972 United Press International item on the reappearance of three of Saloth Sar's aides — Khieu Samphan, Hou Youn, and Hu Nim — believed dead for five years. The Khmer Rouge proved expert in such deceptions, including the cloaking of Saloth Sar's role as the party's political and military leader.

ADVANCE FOR AMS THURSDAY 1/27/72. FOR USE WITH "GHOSTS" STORY BY BORIS BACZYNSKY NXP1728505-1/27/72-PHNOM PENH: Apparently recent photographs appear to show that three prominent Cambodian leftists, believed by many to have been killed five years ago, are in fact alive and living in guerrilla-controlled area of Cambodia. The three are (L-R):Khieu Samphan, Hou Youn and Houhnim, National Assemblymen who disappeared mysteriously from here in 1967.The pictures show each man separately, sitting at a table smiling. (UPI) we

ment collectors at reduced prices. The ramassage system was first introduced in Battambang Province in the northwest, then the center of rice production.

It was not a popular measure. Outraged peasants rose up in vigorous demonstrations of protest, some spontaneous and some organized by the Communists. Soldiers were attacked. The climax occurred in the village of Samlaut, where two soldiers who had been assigned to collect the rice were murdered by the peasants. A crowd of about 200 peasants then armed themselves with the soldiers' guns, took up banners with anti-U.S. and anti–Lon Nol slogans that had been prepared by the local Communists, and attacked a provincial army guard post.

The incident at Samlaut created such a furor in Phnom Penh that Lon Nol had to resign. He was replaced as prime minister by Son Sann, a member of his cabinet, and then by Penn Nouth. But Lon Nol was not gone long; he would reassume the prime ministership in 1969.

Meanwhile, Sihanouk denounced the Communists, accusing them of masterminding the Samlaut massacre. At this time, the principal Communists remaining in the capital were Khieu Samphan, Hou Youn, and Hu Nim, all former members of the Paris study group to which Saloth Sar had belonged. They had managed to coexist with both Sihanouk and Lon Nol and had even held cabinet posts. Now, however, they felt themselves in danger of arrest or worse and left the city, hidden in farmers' carts. Sihanouk claimed that they were dead. When they later popped up among the Khmer Rouge leaders, they were called "the three ghosts."

Unlike Lon Nol and Sihanouk, Saloth Sar and the Khmer Rouge were overjoyed by the incident in Samlaut. To them, the unrest meant that the Cambodian peasantry was ready to support an armed revolt against the government. Saloth Sar seized the opportunity and declared war on Sihanouk.

The prince was determined to crush the Communist opposition within his own country, even while he remained on friendly terms with the

Chinese and Vietnamese Communists. He ordered the army and air force to attack the rebel hideouts and offered rewards to civilians who captured or killed rebels. Saloth Sar decided it was time to move out of the eastern plains into a less accessible stronghold. He selected Ratanakiri Province in the far northeastern corner of the country. Bu Phat was Saloth Sar's aide-de-camp at this time and escorted him on the trip to Ratanakiri.

Ratanakiri is an isolated region. Its principal characteristics are steep, jungle-covered mountains, wild animals, and malaria. Its inhabitants, who live in small, scattered settlements, belong to the dark-skinned highland tribes called the Khmer Leou. The Khmer Leou considered themselves hereditary enemies of the lowland Khmer and especially of city dwellers and the government. They willingly sheltered the Khmer Rouge, and many of them joined it.

For his part, Saloth Sar was impressed with the pride, isolationism, and self-sufficiency of the Khmer Leou. These qualities reinforced an idea that was becoming increasingly important to him: that the revolution must be pure, untainted by materialism, and completely Khmer. Saloth Sar recognized that the extremely difficult conditions of life in the mountains would help the Khmer Rouge believe that they were purified and invincible.

The real fighting began in January 1968. The Khmer Rouge attacked a few army outposts, skirmished with soldiers and police in various parts of the countryside, and captured a couple of artillery guns. Sihanouk and Lon Nol responded promptly. Having found the location of Saloth Sar's hideout, Sihanouk personally led the army in a swift attack. It was a close call for Brother Number One and Brother Number Two, but they escaped with other leaders and set up a new headquarters. About 180 Khmer Leou, who had been given rifles by the Communists, were killed in the attack, and 30 Khmer Rouge were captured; they were promptly executed. "I do not care if I am sent to hell," Sihanouk said in defense of the executions. "I will submit the per-

tinent documents to the devil himself."

Fighting continued over the next several years. The Communists were chiefly interested in raiding police and army posts for guns and building a base of loyalty among the peasantry. Among the propaganda they circulated was the statement that Khieu Samphan, the respected intellectual who still had a following in Phnom Penh, was the leader of the Khmer Rouge; this allowed Saloth Sar to mask his identity and encouraged leftists in the towns to support the Communist rebels.

A group of Khmer Leou tribesmen, who lived on the border between Vietnam and Cambodia. The Khmer Rouge guerrillas lived among the highland warrior tribes, adopted many of their techniques for surviving in the bush, and recruited them to join the fight against the city-based government forces.

Sihanouk saw the conflict as a full-fledged civil war and declared his determination to wipe out the rebels. Knowing that the Khmer Rouge received some supplies and weapons from the North Vietnamese army and often fought side by side with Vietnamese Communist soldiers in both Cambodia and South Vietnam, the prince began to loosen his ties with the Vietnamese toward the end of the 1960s. In 1969, he allowed U.S. bombing of Communist strongholds on Cambodian soil — even though Cambodia and the United States were not

A U.S. Air Force B-52 carpet bombs the Cambodian countryside in 1969. Sihanouk approved the massive raids in an effort to dislodge Vietcong and Khmer Rouge guerrillas from Cambodian territory. One year later the Americans invaded Cambodia; both the bombing and the invasion failed to expel the Communists and resulted in thousands of civilian casualties.

at war — and in early 1970 he demanded a complete withdrawal of Vietnamese troops from the border region.

Yet within the space of a few months, Sihanouk would suddenly switch sides and ally himself with the Khmer Rouge. The events that led to this astonishing turnaround started when Sihanouk went to France for his yearly vacation. He planned to return home by way of Moscow and Beijing. While he was gone, Prime Minister Lon Nol took control of the country in a lightning coup that was encouraged

and possibly aided by the CIA. He instructed the National Assembly to depose Sihanouk as head of state and turn full power over to him as prime minister. He also ordered the airport guarded in case the ousted prince tried to return.

Sihanouk was in Moscow when he learned of the coup. He went on to Beijing as planned and was invited by the Chinese authorities to set up a government-in-exile there. He called it the Royal Government of the National Union of Cambodia, which was known by its French initials: GRUNK.

Back home in Cambodia, Lon Nol called his new regime the Khmer Republic. The United States immediately opened diplomatic relations with the Khmer Republic and gave it $10 million in aid.

Immediately after Sihanouk arrived in Beijing, the Chinese summoned Saloth Sar there. They hoped that Saloth Sar and Sihanouk would set aside their long-standing enmity and unite against Lon Nol. Saloth Sar and Sihanouk did not meet face-to-face at this time, and Saloth Sar's identity was still kept a secret, but the two did agree to cooperate in a united resistance front, which would be the military arm of GRUNK. On March 23, Sihanouk announced the formation of the National United Front of Cambodia (FUNK), with himself as its public leader.

In some ways, FUNK was an elaborate series of deceptions. The world saw Prince Sihanouk — who was still respected and regarded as the legitimate head of state of Cambodia by many nations — as the front's leader. In reality, however, the front was controlled by the Cambodian Communists of the Khmer Rouge; Sihanouk realized this early and within a few years acknowledged it openly. Another level of deception concerned the Khmer Rouge itself. Cambodians and foreigners alike were told that Khieu Samphan was the leader of the Khmer Rouge. But within the movement Brother Number One was recognized as the true leader, and only the central party committee and a few high-ranking cadres knew that Brother Number One was Saloth Sar. The real leader of the Khmer Rouge and of FUNK thus remained concealed from all but a handful of people.

The Lon Nol coup and the surprising alliance with Sihanouk gave new life to the Khmer Rouge. They started receiving substantial amounts of weapons, funds, and other aid from China and North Vietnam. Their numbers also increased, from about 5,000 in 1969 to 35,000 or more in 1974. But Sihanouk had almost nothing to do with the planning or the day-to-day operations of the front. He remained in Beijing, where on frequent visits Ieng

Lieutenant General Lon Nol of the Cambodian army ousted Prince Sihanouk in a 1970 coup backed by the United States. The Americans propped up the staunchly anti-Communist Lon Nol government, which took over the fight against the Khmer Rouge.

Sary acted as a go-between for the prince and Brother Number One.

Only once did Sihanouk join the Khmer Rouge in their jungle camps. The visit was made chiefly for propaganda reasons so that photographs could be taken to assure the outside world that Sihanouk was really in charge of the front. It occurred in the spring of 1973. Sihanouk, his wife, and other members of his group from Beijing traveled from China down the Ho Chi Minh trail, a road through mountains and jungles that the Vietnamese Communists had built to supply their troops in South Vietnam. Like the Khmer Rouge, the royal visitors dressed in black cotton pants and shirts and wore sandals made from old automobile tires. They were photographed sleeping in hammocks in huts and trudg-

Saloth Sar's close aide Khieu Samphan and Sihanouk embrace at a Khmer Rouge camp in northern Cambodia in 1973. After Lon Nol overthrew him, Sihanouk switched his allegiance to the Khmer Rouge. The prince lived in exile in China, which had long supplied the Khmer Rouge with weapons.

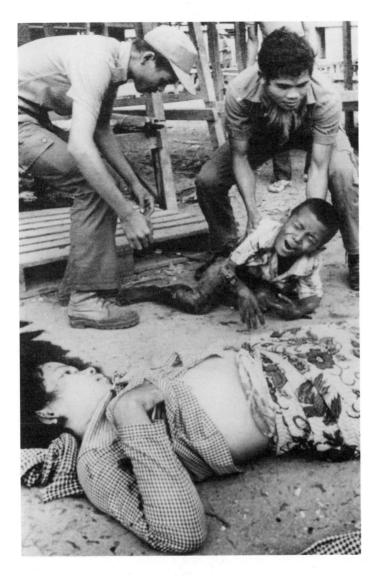

Civilian victims of a Khmer Rouge rocket attack in Phnom Penh, when the guerrillas started a yearlong shelling of the capital. Throughout the early 1970s the Khmer Rouge advanced against the inefficient army of Lon Nol; the Communist successes in Cambodia were mirrored in Vietnam, where the North Vietnamese army and the Vietcong closed in on Saigon as U.S. forces withdrew.

ing along jungle trails. Then they went back to Beijing. Throughout the monthlong visit, Khieu Samphan successfully posed as the leader of the Khmer Rouge; Saloth Sar, it appeared, was merely a military commander.

The Khmer Rouge opposition to the Lon Nol regime grew steadily stronger throughout the early 1970s, and by 1973 the Khmer Rouge controlled significant areas of the countryside. That year they endured 6 months of heavy bombing by American

Khmer Rouge guerrillas enter Phnom Penh in April 1975. When Saloth Sar rode into the captured capital he adopted his final alias, the name by which he would become known to the world as one of history's most notorious mass murderers: Pol Pot.

B-52s, which dropped 539,129 tons of explosives on Cambodia in an attempt to buttress the Khmer Republic. Many civilian towns, villages, and farming areas were hit by American bombs, resulting in a great number of civilian dead and wounded.

One result of the bombing campaign was widespread anger and protest in the United States. In January 1973, the U.S. government had announced its intention to withdraw from South Vietnam; now American antiwar activists demanded a halt to the bombing in Cambodia. The U.S. government, already shaken by the level of domestic opposition to the war, stopped the bombing in August.

As the Khmer Rouge gained military strength and success, it tightened its hold on the countryside. Although the cadres still adhered to the code that prohibited theft or rape, their relationship with the people changed. In all areas controlled by the Khmer Rouge, the farmers and villagers were forced to live and work in collectives — that is, farming communities overseen by Khmer Rouge soldiers. These collectives were fenced and guarded; no one was able to leave or enter without Khmer Rouge permission. The Khmer Rouge forbade the people working in the farming collectives to use the products or crops they produced. Everything was turned over to the cadres, who doled out food and other goods as needed. Mail was stopped, religious activity was banned, and minority groups such as the Chams and Khmer-Vietnamese were persecuted. Most terrifying of all, people soon learned that Angka did not tolerate dissent. Those who criticized the Khmer Rouge or attempted to evade its directives were taken away and did not return. In short, life in the Khmer Rouge collectives was a foretaste of what was to come in Democratic Kampuchea.

At first, not much was known about all this in Phnom Penh or the rest of the world. Then, in 1973, a man named Ith Sarin returned to Phnom Penh after having spent a year with the Khmer Rouge. He had left the capital in disgust at Lon Nol, but he came back filled with dread that what he had seen in the Khmer Rouge collectives might be the country's future. He wrote a book called *Regrets for the Khmer Soul*, which was filled with useful information about the Khmer Rouge. Although the book became something of a best-seller in Phnom Penh, it was disregarded by both the Americans and Lon Nol. Had the world paid more attention to Ith Sarin's warnings and to the stories told by the refugees who swarmed into the capital from the countryside, it might have been less stunned by the tragedy that later unfolded in Democratic Kampuchea.

Lon Nol's government, meanwhile, was rotten with corruption from top to bottom, and the Khmer Republic army was inefficient and often bloodthirsty. Lon Nol himself, a pure-blooded Khmer who liked his soldiers to call him Black Papa in reference to his dark Khmer skin, maintained that the Khmer were racially superior to the neighboring peoples. He persecuted and massacred minorities, especially the Vietnamese; he also wanted to make Cambodia an all-Buddhist country and to that end persecuted the sizable population of Roman Catholics and the Muslim Chams.

After the United States withdrew its bombing support of the Khmer Republic in August 1973, the outcome of the war was never really in doubt. The Khmer Rouge began shelling Phnom Penh in January 1974. They besieged the capital in January 1975. In April 1975 the city fell to the Khmer Rouge, and Saloth Sar rode into the city and adopted his final alias.

This was the birth of Pol Pot.

7

The Corpses in the Killing Fields

Pol Pot quickly put Angka in charge of the country, with himself in charge of Angka — although his identity still remained a secret to the vast majority of Cambodians. A new constitution was introduced in January 1976, renaming the country Democratic Kampuchea (D.K.) and setting up a government that was a front for the CPK. Soon thereafter, the mutually mistrustful alliance between Prince Sihanouk and the Communists broke down.

Sihanouk had returned to Phnom Penh in September 1976 and had been named its official head of state. He set off on an international tour to gain recognition for the new state, and with his help, Democratic Kampuchea won a seat in the United Nations. But in April 1976, after returning from his tour, he formally resigned as head of state — perhaps under duress — and was placed under house arrest by Pol Pot.

That same month, the CPK elected Pol Pot prime minister and Khieu Samphan head of state of Democratic Kampuchea. Sihanouk and his wife spent the next few years as prisoners, their contacts with

Pol Pot in 1978, as premier of Democratic Kampuchea. Under the Pol Pot regime Cambodia was turned into a vast concentration camp in which 1 million to 2 million people perished. Cambodians today refer to the brief but unimaginably bloody era as the "Pol Pot time."

Pol Pot stands in the lead car of a motorcade carrying him through Beijing's Tiananmen Square during his 1977 state visit to China, one of only two foreign trips he made as head of state. China was the Khmer Rouge's strongest backer in the 1960s and 1970s and remained so throughout the 1980s.

the rest of the world limited to a radio and occasional visits from Khieu Samphan. A dozen or so members of their family — children and grandchildren — disappeared during that time and are believed to have been killed by the Khmer Rouge.

Pol Pot remained prime minister throughout all of the Democratic Kampuchea era. According to D.K. records, he also occupied a seat in the new party legislature, which was called the People's Representative Assembly, where he represented the union of rubber plantation workers; nothing is known of his connection with this group or of his activities in the assembly.

Democratic Kampuchea's international relations were almost nonexistent. Pol Pot made only two state visits, to Hanoi and Beijing, both in 1977. With the exception of a few Chinese and European journalists who were invited to tour the country as part of a propaganda effort, foreigners were forbidden to enter Democratic Kampuchea. Those who did were usually tortured and then executed. Among them was a 35-year-old American yachtsman named James Clark, whose sailboat strayed into Cambodian waters; he perished in the Tuol Sleng incarceration center in Phnom Penh. Better known is the case of the *Mayaguez*, an American merchant ship that sailed past an offshore island in May 1975 and was seized by the Khmer Rouge navy. U.S. president Gerald Ford sent a force of American marines to attack the Cambodian coast and recapture the ship; the mission succeeded, but American losses were heavy.

For the most part, however, Democratic Kampuchea had little contact with the outside world and sought none, but it did have a great deal of trouble with Vietnam, its neighbor to the east. The North Vietnamese succeeded in capturing Saigon just days after the Khmer Rouge took Phnom Penh, and they immediately unified North Vietnam and South Vietnam under a single Communist government. Almost before the smoke of battle had cleared over Phnom Penh and Saigon, Cambodia and Vietnam began arguing over border territories. China and the Soviet Union, the two Communist superpowers, were indirectly involved in the dispute, China backing Cambodia and the Soviet Union backing Vietnam. By 1977, skirmishing between the Khmer Rouge and the Vietnamese army had escalated into a new war.

The political history of Pol Pot's regime can be summarized in a few paragraphs, but its human

U.S. marines shortly after recapturing the American merchant ship *Mayaguez*, which had been seized by the forces of Pol Pot's regime when the ship strayed into Cambodian waters. The 39-man crew of the ship was rescued in the 1975 commando operation, but 38 marines were killed by Khmer Rouge defenders.

history is not so easily told. The compelling interest that Democratic Kampuchea holds for people around the world today lies in the intensity of the misery it brought to the Cambodians, in the sheer numbers of those who died — and in the gruesome paradox of a leader who seemed bent on destroying his own people.

Since the early 1980s, scores of books and articles have told the stories of Cambodians who lived through the nightmare of Democratic Kampuchea. Many of these survivors' stories begin the same way: with the evacuation of Phnom Penh.

Pol Pot did not just want to take over the country as it had existed under Sihanouk and Lon Nol. He had nothing less in mind than the complete restructuring of Cambodian society to conform to his political ideals — a forcible restructuring, if necessary. He envisioned a Cambodia covered with collective villages like those the Khmer Rouge had established in the countryside, a Cambodia that would be entirely self-sufficient, supporting itself on its rice crop and producing the goods it needed in its own workshops and factories. Cities had no place in this vision, and he wanted them emptied.

On the day the Khmer Rouge marched into Phnom Penh, they gave its citizens the order to march out. The experience of Haing Ngor, a Phnom Penh doctor, was typical: Armed teenage Khmer Rouge soldiers burst into the hospital where he was operating on a wounded soldier and ordered everyone to leave at once. The unconscious soldier was left lying on the surgical table. Patients who could walk were ordered into the streets; some were made to carry their own beds. Methodically, every building in the city was emptied, and a vast, slow-moving, confused crowd filled the streets and began shuffling toward the outbound highways. Those who resisted were shot. So was anyone who was identified as a Lon Nol soldier or a member of the previous government. Many people were separated from their families, and most had time to gather only a few possessions.

Haing Ngor and other survivors report that the city dwellers seemed dazed. They thought that the

The Khmer Rouge would have been nothing but a half-forgotten, ragged band of guerrillas in the hills if it hadn't been for the 1970 coup. When Sihanouk was overthrown, and then unexpectedly joined them as a figurehead, the Khmer Rouge became politically significant overnight.
—HAING NGOR
Cambodian refugee

A pistol-brandishing Khmer Rouge soldier rounds up shopkeepers during the capture of Phnom Penh on April 17, 1975. That day the entire population of the city — more than 1 million people — was rounded up and marched into the countryside.

war was over. What, then, did this ominous forced march mean? One incident witnessed by Haing Ngor seemed to herald a future of despair. As he crossed a bridge over the Bassac River, he saw a shiny new Peugeot automobile being driven down the bank and into the water. The man, woman, and children inside it stared out the car's windows, and the doors and windows remained shut as the car slowly sank. Haing Ngor realized at once that he had just seen a rich family committing suicide.

It took days for the Khmer Rouge to clear Phnom Penh. Upon reaching the countryside, the people were told that they must all return to their native villages. Those who had no villages would be relocated by Angka. For hundreds of thousands of Cambodians, life in Democratic Kampuchea would be a seemingly endless series of relocations, forced marches, and separations.

Once settled in a village, temporary camp, or collective, people learned what they were supposed to do: work. Everyone must labor for Angka, whether in the rice paddies or digging ditches. To refuse, to demand a choice, meant to die. "The Pol Pot soldiers never killed people in front of us," said Mey Komphot, a banker who was driven into slave labor in the fields. "They politely asked them to come. No one ever returned." One phrase used by the soldiers and cadres on such occasions was, "The plastic bag awaits." This was a reference to the bags in which bodies were buried after executions — until the regime ran out of bags and began simply tipping the corpses into pits in what were called the killing fields. To conserve valuable ammunition, victims were often ordered to kneel at the edges of the pits and were then struck at the base of the neck with metal bars.

The evacuees from Phnom Penh and other cities soon learned something else about the new society Pol Pot had created. Although the rhetoric of revolution had called for the elimination of social classes, there were three very distinct classes under Angka.

The first was the organization itself, consisting of the CPK cadres and the Khmer Rouge soldiers. The rest of the population was divided into two classes: the "base people," or "old people," and the "new people." The base people were the mountain people and rural peasants who had supported or been sympathetic to the Khmer Rouge during its years of struggle. Most of them were poor and uneducated, and as a group they were resentful of urbanites and intellectuals. The new people were all those who had come from the cities and towns. Individuals who had been educated (or wore eye-

Cambodians toil in rice paddies in 1978 under forced labor. Countless Cambodians perished during years of dawn-to-dusk labor, always under the threat of the death penalty for such minor infractions as failing to turn over to guards a piece of fruit found beneath a tree. Laborers, usually forced to sleep in the open for a few hours each night, rarely had more than one meager meal a day.

glasses, which were considered a symbol of education), who spoke foreign languages, or who had held professional jobs in such areas as teaching and medicine quickly discovered that their chances of survival would improve if they disguised themselves as illiterate peasants.

The new people were subservient to the base people, who, after a long history of being downtrodden and ignored, were more than happy to vent their frustrations on the new arrivals. The base people supervised work gangs made up of the new people and reserved the best food and other supplies for themselves. They also held long sessions of political indoctrination at which the new people were required to criticize themselves and inform on their fellows. Periodic purges — that is, mass executions intended to purify the group — were carried out in the collectives. New people whose loyalty to Angka was suspect usually disappeared — and disloyalty could consist of something as simple as eating a piece of fruit found in the forest instead of turning it over to Angka.

> *Angka has as many eyes as a pineapple and cannot make mistakes.*
> —Khmer Rouge saying

Pol Pot wanted Democratic Kampuchea to be a completely new society, his own brave new world. Every link to the past was severed. Traditional dances and costumes were banned. The old names of provinces and regions were abolished; the country was divided into zones, and place-names were replaced with numbers. Religion was completely outlawed. Money was done away with, and the private ownership of any sort of property was forbidden. In the eyes of the regime, the people needed nothing but food and clothing, which would be provided by Angka. Temples were destroyed, statues were melted down, and monks were forced to work in the fields and killed if they resisted. Angkor Wat, which had already suffered some damage in the war, was shelled and vandalized by the Khmer Rouge. Further damage to Angkor was done by some of the Cambodians who fled to Thailand to escape the Khmer Rouge; they knocked the heads from statues and sold or bartered them at the border.

Perhaps the greatest casualty of Democratic Kampuchea was ordinary family life. Not only were many

Women in a Khmer Rouge indoctrination center. An inescapable stream of propaganda and indoctrination was a constant feature of all activities under Pol Pot right from the Year Zero, which was what the Khmer Rouge ordered everyone to call 1975, the year of Pol Pot's takeover.

families across the country torn apart by Angka's program of forced relocation, but families were unable to remain together in the collectives. Young children were taken from their parents to be trained by cadres; they were said to be Angka's property. Men and women were housed in separate barracks. Married couples could see one another only with Angka's permission, and unmarried couples could marry only on Angka's orders. To be discovered in any sort of sexual relationship outside this framework meant death.

Throughout the D.K. era, Phnom Penh was a ghost town, empty but for high-ranking party officers and their families. Pol Pot lived there; it is said that he kept many houses and moved around constantly to avoid assassination. Ieng Sary and Khieu Tirith lived there as well. Khieu Ponnary, Pol Pot's wife, was kept under guard in a residence of her own in Phnom Penh. She had begun to suffer a serious mental breakdown during the 1960s, and by the time the Khmer Rouge won the war, she was completely insane. Her present whereabouts and status are unknown.

Pol Pot's ambitious attempt to create a self-sufficient Cambodian nation failed. The failure became apparent early in the D.K. years, when food shortages were widespread and starvation stalked the land. Angka ordered many thousands of people to build dams and canals to irrigate the rice lands, but the workers and supervisors alike were untrained, and the dams gave way at the first rainfall, flooding many villages but leaving the fields without water.

Gasoline, ammunition, medicine, and other goods became scarce; and when goods did exist, they were poorly distributed, so that some regions had surpluses and others shortages. Each economic disaster led to new purges and fresh corpses for the killing fields. By 1977, the base people were being purged along with the new people.

There were military setbacks, too. Every time Cambodia suffered a defeat at the hands of the vastly superior Vietnamese forces, the military officials involved were purged. The story of So Phim illustrates how Pol Pot's revolution ultimately destroyed many of its own leaders.

So Phim was a longtime member of the CPK central committee and an associate of Pol Pot's and Ieng Sary's. He had a well-earned reputation for cruelty and for unquestioning loyalty to Angka. He was made commander of the Eastern Zone, near the Vietnam border. At first, matters went well in the Eastern Zone, and So Phim was considered the best of the zone commanders. Then he was ordered to attack Vietnam. The attack was not very successful, and 400 soldiers under So Phim's command were called to Phnom Penh, where they were tortured and executed. Pol Pot's security force began to suspect So Phim of being "a Khmer body with a Vietnamese mind," which was Angka jargon for a traitor.

All the evidence shows that So Phim was completely loyal to Angka and Pol Pot. Yet, when he once again failed to win a border battle that had been ordered by Pol Pot, all of his officers were summoned to a meeting with some security officers. They were ambushed and killed. Then, So Phim himself received instructions to attend a meeting with the security officers. He sent a messenger to ask what the meeting was to be about. When the messenger failed to return, he sent a second, then a third and a fourth. None came back.

So Phim still could not believe that Pol Pot meant to kill him. He went into hiding and petitioned Pol Pot for a personal interview. Pol Pot agreed to meet with his old comrade, but when So Phim showed up, he was greeted by two boatloads of security police. He shot himself before they could get to him.

Skulls in a Cambodian killing field, some still bearing the blindfolds used during the execution. Thousands were executed for crimes ranging from the violation of minor work rules to being wealthy, being a doctor or some other professional, or even for wearing glasses, which the Khmer Rouge believed was evidence of being an intellectual. Ten years after the expulsion of the Khmer Rouge, fields of skulls and bones could still be found throughout Cambodia.

His wife and children were killed while they tried to bury him. One of So Phim's aides managed to escape into the jungle and eventually made his way to Vietnam. His name was Heng Samrin; the Vietnamese made him president of Cambodia after the fall of the Pol Pot regime.

Whether the issue was dams that would not hold, rice that would not grow, or enemies that would not be defeated, Pol Pot seemed unable to admit that any of his plans had failed. It was a characteristic of Democratic Kampuchea that whenever one of Angka's schemes went awry, a scapegoat — or a few thousand scapegoats — would be found and punished. The logic ran this way: Pol Pot's ideas cannot be wrong; therefore, there must be traitors among the people. The solution to every problem was more killing. By 1978, party cadres were being purged along with base people and new people, and terror and suspicion were omnipresent.

The source of the terror and suspicion was a building in Phnom Penh, on the grounds of what had formerly been a school. This building was now the incarceration center of Angka's security police. Its official D.K. designation was S.21, but today it is called Tuol Sleng, which means "hill of the poison tree." To be arrested by Tuol Sleng officers was the most dreaded fate in Democratic Kampuchea.

About 20,000 Cambodians were executed at Tuol Sleng, usually after torture. Most of them were party

A drawing of prisoners shackled to the floor in a room at S.21 Incarceration Center, a school that the Khmer Rouge converted into an interrogation and torture center where some 20,000 people were executed. This drawing was made by Heng Nath, a prisoner who was later executed.

cadres. They were forced to write "confessions" claiming that they had acted as spies for Vietnam or the CIA. These documents were carefully preserved, as were the photographs that were taken of the victims before and after death.

One of the most remarkable features of Democratic Kampuchea is that the rest of the world knew so little about it at the time. Pol Pot's hostility to foreigners and his deliberate isolationism built a wall of silence around Cambodia. Only when the stories told by Cambodian refugees at the Thailand border began to filter into the press did the world wake up to what was going on. Even then, many found it difficult to believe that such horrifying accounts could be true. Some leftists in the United States and other countries maintained that press treatment of Democratic Kampuchea was exaggerated in order to discredit communism; most of them later changed their views when abundant proof of Pol Pot's Cambodian genocide came to the surface.

At the end of the 1970s, Pol Pot's great experiment in social restructuring was collapsing under the weight of famine, despair, and war. By that time, however, Vietnam was preparing to bring the experiment to an end.

Photographs of some of those killed at S.21. The Khmer Rouge meticulously recorded the details of each prisoner's interrogation, torture, and death in photographs and transcripts. S.21 is now called Tuol Sleng (Hill of the Poison Tree) and is a permanent memorial to those who died at the hands of the Pol Pot regime.

8

Return to the Jungle

Vietnam invaded Cambodia on December 25, 1978. It was no border skirmish; the Vietnamese force consisted of 14 divisions of troops and full bomb and gunnery support from the air force. To the world, Vietnam claimed that it had decided to end Pol Pot's monstrous regime — in other words, that the invasion had a humanitarian basis. No one was fooled, however. Sincere though the Vietnamese may have been in wanting to depose Pol Pot, it is probable that their main object was to get their hands on Cambodia at last.

The Vietnamese army easily quelled the resistance it encountered on its way to the capital from the disorganized and demoralized Khmer Rouge. By January 5, gunfire and mortar shelling could be heard in Phnom Penh.

That night, Pol Pot came to the residence where Prince Sihanouk had been under house arrest since April 1976. To Sihanouk's astonishment, Pol Pot apologized in his mild voice for having been too busy to meet with him sooner, and then he asked Sihanouk to appear at the United Nations on behalf of

Cambodia did not exist anymore. Atomic bombs could not have destroyed more of it than civil war and communism.
—HAING NGOR
Cambodian refugee, on the state of Cambodia in 1979

Pol Pot in a Khmer Rouge jungle stronghold in December 1979, shortly after his regime had been ousted by the invading Vietnamese army. Expelled after less than five years of rapacious rule, Pol Pot and his forces returned to the countryside to fight a new guerrilla war.

Troops of the Vietnamese army entering Phnom Penh in January 1979. The invasion of Cambodia by the Soviet-backed Vietnamese, in which they ousted the Chinese-backed Khmer Rouge, was an extension of the rivalry between the two Communist superpowers. Vietnam also acted out of revulsion toward Pol Pot's regime and out of ancient ethnic enmity between the Vietnamese and Khmer peoples.

Democratic Kampuchea. Sihanouk agreed, perhaps because he felt that representing his Khmer Rouge captors would be preferable to turning the country's UN seat over to the Vietnamese invaders, perhaps he was simply looking for a way out of the war zone. Pol Pot released him, and Sihanouk flew out of Cambodia and into another period of exile. After a stop at UN headquarters in New York City, where he denounced the Vietnamese invasion, he once more took up residence in Beijing.

As the Vietnamese advanced, Pol Pot and the Khmer Rouge retreated northward, into the mountain regions that had sheltered them during the Lon Nol years. They had stocked some of their old camps with caches of food and other supplies. But the Vietnamese were more successful than Lon Nol had been at scouring the countryside, and many of the Khmer Rouge were forced to flee across the Thailand border. There, ironically, they set up refugee camps of their own, cheek by jowl with those Cambodians who had fled Democratic Kampuchea. To outsiders, the camps and the refugees looked identical, but Cambodians could tell the difference: The Khmer Rouge refugees were well fed and seemed healthy, while nearly everyone who had fled from Pol Pot seemed to be starving and ill.

Not all of the Khmer Rouge went to Thailand. Some were killed in the fighting; others simply settled into the countryside and passed themselves off as peasants; some of the senior cadres went to China. Pol Pot, Ieng Sary, and Khieu Samphan were among the last group. Like Sihanouk, they established themselves in Beijing.

The victorious Vietnamese set up a new government in Cambodia; it was the type of regime that is called a puppet government, because its leaders were controlled by the Vietnamese. Under this regime, Cambodia was renamed the People's Republic of Kampuchea (PRK). Heng Samrin, the aide of So Phim's who had defected to Vietnam, was appointed president. In the late 1980s, his role as leader has been overshadowed by that of Prime Minister Hun Sen, also a former Khmer Rouge officer who defected to Vietnam. In the spring of 1989, Hun Sen announced that the name of the country had been changed once again, this time to the State of Cambodia; this move was probably an attempt to distance his government from the name Kampuchea, which has come to be associated with Pol Pot.

The PRK has been unable to dislodge Democratic Kampuchea from Cambodia's seat in the United Nations. Nor has it won diplomatic recognition from the United States, which has not acknowledged the

Cambodian refugees fleeing over the border to Thailand in 1975. Throughout the 1970s and 1980s, wave after wave of refugees fled the Americans, the North and South Vietnamese, the armies of Lon Nol and Pol Pot, the privations of the Khmer Rouge regime, and finally the full-scale Vietnamese invasion.

A statue in the town of Neak Luong marking the Vietnamese expulsion of the Khmer Rouge. The Vietnamese-installed rulers normalized life in Cambodia, but most nations refused to recognize the new government. Some nations, including China and the United States, continued to recognize Pol Pot's regime as the legitimate government of Cambodia.

legitimacy of any government in Cambodia since Lon Nol's fall from power. For nearly a decade, Vietnam supported the PRK with about 200,000 troops from the Vietnamese army that were stationed in Cambodia. The United States and other nations continued to claim that the presence of these troops constituted an illegal military occupation, and they refused to trade with Vietnam or provide foreign aid until the troops were withdrawn. Finally, bowing to world opinion, Vietnam withdrew its troops in the fall of 1989 and left the PRK to stand on its own.

Many of the Cambodian refugees were almost as opposed to the PRK as they had been to Democratic Kampuchea, but the Vietnam-backed government has introduced some positive changes in Cambodian life. The ban on Buddhism was lifted, and the temples and temple schools were allowed to reopen, although only a fraction of the prewar population of monks remained alive. Efforts have been under way to repair the war damage in Phnom Penh, which again houses a large population. Although the economy is technically based on the Communist model and thus controlled by the state, free-market enterprise is permitted on a small scale. Farmers may now keep what they grow, and shopkeepers, vendors, and restaurateurs operate without much interference from the government. With the help of archaeologists and technicians from India, some restoration work has been done at Angkor Wat. Traditional clothing, dance, arts, and customs are allowed to flourish. And the PRK has turned Angka's old incarceration center into the Tuol Sleng Museum of the Genocidal Crimes of Pol Pot. The "confessions" and photographs of the prisoners are on display there, as are the electrified bed frames that were the regime's torture racks.

Opposition to the PRK regime is presented by a resistance movement that includes both Pol Pot and Sihanouk. This movement—a classic case of politics making strange bedfellows—was born in China in the years immediately following the Vietnamese invasion.

At first, Sihanouk and the Khmer Rouge leaders declared separately that they would continue to oppose the PRK through both international diplomacy and guerrilla warfare. Sihanouk would have nothing to do with the Khmer Rouge, nor they with him.

Remains of victims found in Cheung Ek village; the iron manacles used on the victims hang from a bar at left. In the 1980s the survivors of the Pol Pot time suffered enormous psychological traumas, which were eased in part by the restoration of traditional Buddhism. All over the country monks could be seen praying over piles of skulls and bones.

The prince founded a resistance group called the National United Front for an Independent, Neutral, Peaceful, and Cooperative Cambodia (FUNCINPEC). Its military arm — numbering about 7,000 soldiers and guerrilla fighters — is called the Armée Nationale Sihanoukienne (ANS). A third resistance group also entered the picture. It is the Khmer People's National Liberation Front (KPNLF), led by Son Sann, who had been part of the old Lon Nol government.

China, which wanted Vietnam out of Cambodia, provided support for all three resistance movements, but it soon became apparent that the different groups were competing for resources and publicity. In 1982, Chinese officials persuaded them to join in a coalition that was supposed to last only until the PRK was overthrown. The organization that resulted is called the Coalition Government of Democratic Kampuchea (CGDK). Sihanouk is the prime minister of the CGDK, Son Sann is its president, and Khieu Samphan is its vice-president for foreign affairs. For the second time in their stormy history, Sihanouk and Pol Pot have been forced into an alliance against a common enemy.

At the close of the 1980s, the United States and other third parties were busy trying to arrange a settlement between the CGDK and the PRK. Various schemes were discussed, including power sharing

In Beijing in 1985, Chinese president Li Xiannian (second from right) hosts the leaders of the three guerrilla factions fighting the Vietnam-backed Cambodian government that ousted Pol Pot. The leaders of the allied factions are, from left, Son Sann, Prince Sihanouk, and Khieu Samphan. Pol Pot, officially retired, was widely believed to still be leading the Khmer Rouge army.

and internationally supervised elections, but the settlement talks broke down in the summer of 1989, when the PRK refused to recognize the Khmer Rouge in any settlement; at the same time, the CGDK — with U.S. backing — announced that it would not participate in a settlement that did not include the Khmer Rouge. As of 1989, the resistance forces were continuing to engage in fighting with the PRK army (and occasionally with each other, as animosity among the three groups still runs very high). The fighting is heaviest in Siem Reap and Battambang provinces, near the Thailand border. Each of the three resistance groups operates refugee camps and guerrilla bases for its own loyalists along the border.

Little is known about Pol Pot's activities during the 1980s. He did not remain in Beijing, as Sihanouk has done, but returned to Cambodia to lead the guerrilla effort. Although he held no official position in the CGDK, he was the military commander of its forces in the field.

During the early 1980s, as the world became more familiar with the horrors of Democratic Kampu-

Well-equipped Khmer Rouge guerrillas in northern Cambodia in the mid-1980s. The Khmer Rouge was the largest of the three allied factions fighting the Vietnamese army, which remained in Cambodia until the end of 1989. In early 1990 the Khmer Rouge captured Cambodia's second largest city, Battambang and gleefully announced that it was "in flames."

Two men who escaped the Pol Pot regime, photographer Dith Pran (later of the *New York Times*) and physician Haing S. Ngor (later an actor in the film *The Killing Fields*) flank writer Elie Weisel, a survivor of the Nazi concentration camps, at the 1988 founding of a human rights group pledged to bringing Pol Pot and the Khmer Rouge to trial for genocide.

chea, people everywhere spoke out in condemnation of Pol Pot. By 1985, the leaders of the Khmer Rouge — quite possibly including Pol Pot himself — had decided that it was time to dissociate the movement from the individual who was so universally reviled. As a result, the Khmer Rouge announced in that year that Pol Pot had officially retired as military commander to become director of something called the Higher Institute for National Defense, about which nothing at all is known.

Since that time, Ieng Sary and Khieu Samphan have been the most visible representatives of the Khmer Rouge on the international stage. Khieu Samphan is the movement's official head today, but many political analysts believe that Pol Pot still wields considerable power in the Khmer Rouge, and some Cambodians fear that he may be directing Khieu Samphan's moves from behind the scenes and possibly even plotting a return to power. Pol Pot is very seldom seen — there have even been rumors that he is dead, but none of them have been confirmed. In the fall of 1989, he was rumored to be living in the Cambodian town of Trat, near the border with Thailand. A human rights organization called the Cambodian Documentation Commission, of which refugees Dith Pran and Haing Ngor are members, is leading an international movement to put the Khmer Rouge on trial for genocide and would like to see Pol Pot face charges in the World Court.

It is difficult to assess the effects of Pol Pot's rule on Cambodia, partly because of the enormity of his actions and partly because the figures for the prewar population and the dead and missing are simply estimates. The prewar population of the country is generally agreed to have been about 7.3 million, and Amnesty International, one of the most respected human rights groups, says that at least 1 million died in the civil war that led up to the Khmer Rouge takeover in 1975 and that between 1 million and 2 million more died in Democratic Kampuchea under Pol Pot. There is no reliable way to determine how many of the deaths were due to murder or execution and how many to disease or starvation.

Cambodia's population was reduced not just by war, murder, and disease but by the exodus of refugees who made their way out of the country. Some, like Heng Samrin, went to Vietnam, but most — like Dith Pran, Haing Ngor, and Someth May, whose stories have become well known — had had enough

A Khmer Rouge—controlled refugee camp on the Thailand side of the Thai-Cambodian border in 1985; it was one of several camps, controlled by various factions, holding more than 250,000 Cambodian refugees. By 1990, some of the camps had been inhabited for so long that they resembled cities, with paved streets and permanent buildings.

105

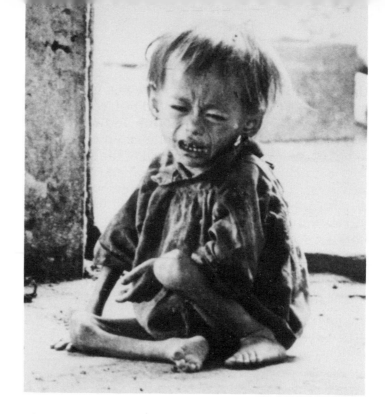

Despite international condemnation and the implementation of a United Nations—sponsored cease-fire plan, Khmer Rouge forces were on the offensive as the 1990s began. For the people of Cambodia, the unspeakable horrors of the Pol Pot time loomed on the horizon once again.

of communism and went to Thailand. Before 1978, escape attempts were extremely dangerous; anyone who tried to leave the country and was caught was likely to be executed. But as the war between Vietnam and Cambodia intensified, Angka's attention turned more and more eastward, and more refugees were able to reach the border. Furthermore, many Cambodians were terrified of the Vietnamese, whom they regarded as hereditary enemies. They had had enough of war, so they left when the Vietnamese arrived. For this reason, the flood of refugees was greatest in 1979 and the early 1980s.

Some of the refugees were fortunate enough to be admitted at once into Thailand or some other country, but by far the greater number of them had to settle into camps along the border, waiting to receive papers that would give them the status of political refugees. All told, at least half a million people left Cambodia between 1975 and 1985. About 200,000 of them were resettled in North America and Europe. A much smaller number have relocated to Asian nations. But at least 250,000 are living in camps near the Thailand-Cambodia border. One-tenth of these refugees live in camps run by the

United Nations; the remainder live in a geopolitical no-man's-land, in camps operated by factions of the CGDK, without UN refugee status and with no effective national identity. Despite international aid and volunteer efforts, people in all of the camps suffer from disease; from shortages of food, medicine, and teachers; and from pervasive depression and other psychological disorders.

A decade after the overthrow of Democratic Kampuchea, Pol Pot remains paradoxical, as enigmatic a figure as ever. Those who know him talk of his quiet voice, his smile, his polite manner, and his small, delicate hands. But some of the surviving victims of Democratic Kampuchea have said that he appears in their nightmares as a giant, faceless demon — the aspect that he presented to them while they lived under his rule. Since his student days he has been adept at secrecy; his life has been constructed of aliases and false fronts. The real Saloth Sar may be unknowable.

Many attempts have been made to explain his actions. Some people say he is simply evil; others theorize that he is insane, perhaps suffering from paranoid delusions; still others suggest that the stress caused by years of constant oppression and struggle made him overreact when he finally came to power. It seems clear that his dedication to his political principles was sincere and that he has never been motivated by greed for personal wealth or fame. But at what point did the earnest young student, the forward-thinking boulevard politician of Paris, harden into the implacable tyrant? How much did he know or care about the fate of individuals in Democratic Kampuchea? Did he believe up to the end that Tuol Sleng and the killing fields were a necessary part of the revolution to which he had dedicated his life? Or was absolute, autocratic power his goal all along?

These questions cannot be answered. It is possible that little more will ever be known about Pol Pot than what is known today. He will go down in history as one of the cruelest and most destructive leaders the world has ever seen — and as one of the most mysterious.

Further Reading

Becker, Elizabeth. *When the War Was Over: The Voices of Cambodia's Revolution and Its People.* New York: Simon & Schuster, 1987.

Canesso, Claudia. *Cambodia.* New York: Chelsea House, 1989.

Chandler, David. *A History of Cambodia.* Boulder, CO: Westview Press, 1983.

Etcheson, Craig. *The Rise and Demise of Democratic Kampuchea.* Boulder, CO: Westview Press, 1984.

Herz, Martin F. *A Short History of Cambodia.* New York: Praeger, 1967.

Kiernan, Ben. *How Pol Pot Came to Power: A History of Communism in Kampuchea, 1930–1975.* London: Verso, 1985.

Mam, Teeda Butt. *To Destroy You Is No Loss: The Odyssey of a Cambodian Family.* New York: Atlantic Monthly Press, 1987.

May, Someth. *Cambodian Witness: An Autobiography of Someth May.* New York: Random House, 1987.

Ngor, Haing, and Roger Warner. *A Cambodian Odyssey.* New York: Warner Books, 1989.

Osborne, Milton E. *Before Kampuchea: Preludes to Tragedy.* Boston: Allen & Unwin, 1984.

Shawcross, William. *The Quality of Mercy: Cambodia, Holocaust, and Modern Conscience.* New York: Simon & Schuster, 1984.

Sihanouk, Norodom. *War and Hope: The Case for Cambodia.* Translated by Mary Feeney. New York: Pantheon Books, 1980.

Stuart-Fox, Martin. *The Murderous Revolution: Life and Death in Pol Pot's Kampuchea.* New York: Alternative Publishers, 1986.

Szymusiak, Molyda. *The Stones Cry Out: A Cambodian Childhood, 1975–1980.* Translated by Linda Coverdale. New York: Hill & Wang, 1986.

Vickery, Michael. *Cambodia 1975–1982.* Boston: South End Press, 1984.

Williams, Marilyn. *The Land in Between: The Cambodian Dilemma.* New York: Morrow, 1970.

Chronology

1928	Born Saloth Sar in Kompong Thom province, Cambodia
1949	Attends technical school in Paris; writes political articles under the pen name "Original Khmer"
1953	Returns to Cambodia; France grants full independence to Cambodia
1955	King Norodom Sihanouk gives up the throne to become prime minister of Cambodia
1960	Cambodian Communists form Workers Party of Kampuchea
1963	Under the pseudonym "Brother Number One," Saloth Sar is elected secretary of Workers Party of Kampuchea; he and other Communists flee Phnom Penh for jungle camps
1963–65	Khmer Rouge Communist resistance force takes shape, with Saloth Sar as leader; Workers Party is renamed Communist Party of Kampuchea
1967	Armed antigovernment riots in the countryside spur open declaration of war on Sihanouk by Khmer Rouge
1969	U.S. bombs Communist bases in Cambodian countryside
1970	In a U.S.-supported coup, General Lon Nol overthrows Sihanouk and establishes the Khmer Republic
1973	U.S. bombs guerrilla and civilian sites in Cambodia from February through August
1974	Khmer Rouge forces besiege Phnom Penh
1975	On April 17, Phnom Penh falls to the Khmer Rouge; Saloth Sar, using the name Pol Pot, takes control and renames the country Democratic Kampuchea
1977	Makes his only state visits, to China and North Korea; war breaks out between Cambodia and Vietnam
1979	Vietnamese forces capture Phnom Penh and topple the Democratic Kampuchea regime; a Vietnam-backed regime renames the country the People's Republic of Kampuchea; Pol Pot flees to China
1982	Khmer Rouge, Sihanouk's forces, and remnants of Lon Nol regime join to oppose the Vietnamese occupation; Pol Pot commands Khmer Rouge from jungle camps
1985	Retires from military command of Khmer Rouge
1989	Vietnamese troops withdraw from Cambodia; peace talks between the People's Republic of Kampuchea and the opposition forces break down

Index

Rebecca Stefoff holds a Ph.D. in English from the University of Pennsylvania, where she taught from 1974 to 1977. A Philadelphia-based editor and writer, she is the author of numerous works of nonfiction, including several biographies for young adults.

Arthur M. Schlesinger, jr., taught history at Harvard for many years and is currently Albert Schweitzer Professor of the Humanities at City University of New York. He is the author of numerous highly praised works in American history and has twice been awarded the Pulitzer Prize. He served in the White House as special assistant to Presidents Kennedy and Johnson.